POSNER THOUGHTS
annotated

PIXIE

POSNER THOUGHTS
annotated

VOLUME 1

by @Posner_Thoughts & Jack Metzler

Introduction by Richard A. Posner

INTERALIAS
Washington, D.C.
2017

Copyright © 2017
Posner_Thoughts, Jack Metzler, interAlias Press
Introduction copyright 2017 Richard A. Posner
All rights reserved
Edited by Jack Metzler
Cover photo by John Gress/Reuters
Photo of Pixie Posner used with her permission.

ISBN: 0991116348
ISBN-13: 978-0991116348
First Edition 2017
Includes bibliographical references and index.

To Dinah and Pixie.

The mighty one salutes you, and welcomes you as a High Priest of Posner Worship.

– Richard A. Posner
(yearbook inscription)

CONTENTS

	Introduction by Richard A. Posner	v
	Forward	vii
0	READ ME	
1	CALL ME DICK	1
2	I AM NOT A SOUR PUSS	15
3	THE POZE KNOWS	29
4	STOP BABBLING	39
5	HELL IS OTHER JUDGES	53
6	THE SUPREME COURT IS AWFUL	67
7	AN ECONOMIC ANALYSIS OF CATS	81
8	NOT IMPRESSED WITH LAW PROFESSORS	95
9	THIS ARGUMENT, IT'S FEEBLE	103
10	THE ADVERSARY SYSTEM IS OVERRATED	111
11	I BLAME THE LAW CLERKS	125
12	WHAT HORRIBLE STUFF	133

Posner Thoughts, *Annotated*

Appendix: Things that are overrated	143
Bibliography	145
Index	151

ACKNOWLEDGMENTS

The authors wish to thank, first and most of all, Judge Richard A. Posner, without whom this book would make very little sense (if it existed at all, which would be surprising and perplexing), for inspiring this book and for his good-sported agreement to write the introduction. We also must acknowledge Pixie Posner, as fine a Maine Coon as we've ever heard of, for *her* inspiration and for granting permission to use her photo.

@Posner_Thoughts also wishes to acknowledge Ronald Reagan for nominating Judge Posner to the Seventh Circuit, Strom Thurmond, Posner's brethren on the Seventh Circuit, his law clerks past and present, those who have interviewed or covered Posner—especially William Domnarski for his wonderful biography—and the tweeps who follow and engage with @Posner_Thoughts on Twitter, particularly those who consider themselves part of #AppellateTwitter.

Jack Metzler offers his thanks to his family, who put up with a lot. No really, *a lot*.

INTRODUCTION

by Richard A. Posner

When I told my cat Pixie that I was honored to have been asked to write an introduction to a book consisting of my sayings, she smirked, wondering who would be interested in what I have to say? I had to reply (truthfully—if you lie to a cat, it scratches you) that actually I didn't know, but given that there are more than 300 million people in the United States, some of whom are even citizens, surely one or two would be interested. She thought surely not. Pixie ran for President in the November election and is somewhat bitter about the outcome, as she thought it plain, given the other candidates, who abused each other so continuously and convincingly, that this would be the year in which, at last, a cat won the Presidency. A cat named Morris ran in the 1968 and 1972 presidential election campaigns and did well, but fell short. Another cat named Bill ran in 1980 and 1984, losing both times (the cat named Bill who won in 1992 and 1996 was not literally a cat). So: two male cats have run and lost (three have run, if you count Bill Clinton). It's time for a female cat to run! There will be another presidential election in 2020. Let's hear it: "Pixie for President!"

Maybe no one will read this introduction, but I feel I must write it, despite my modesty, for which I am famous, to correct certain errors. For example, on the very screen of the online version, I am called "the smartest man in the world." That of course is true—to deny it would be false modesty, which I abhor—but it implies the possibility (though no more than a possibility) that there is, somewhere, a smartest *woman* in the world, leaving open the possibility, which I would like to see foreclosed *forthwith*, that the smartest woman in the world is smarter than Judge Richard A. Posner!* Let any woman claiming to be *at once* the smartest woman in the world *and* smarter even than the renowned Judge Richard A. Posner the First step forth, identify herself, and enter into a competition with me to determine which of us is in fact smarter and therefore smartest. The stages of our contest, I suggest, should be: imitating cat sounds; writing judicial opinions backward; a boxing match without boxing gloves; estimating the IQs of the Supreme Court Justices in the range 80 to 89; and being first to steal a spittoon from behind the bench of the Supreme Court.

One of the tweets in @Posner_Thoughts compares Judge Posner (I generally speak of myself and to myself in the third person, like all narcissistic egomaniacs) to Wayne Gretsky, who I am told was a great hockey player. Fine. But according to *Wikipedia*, "He was adept at dodging checks from opposing players." Obviously I am superior to Gretsky on that point: If someone gives me a

---

* *Editor's note:* The unfortunate possibility referred to is due to the trend of "gender-neutral" writing, which can lead people to believe that the formerly gender-neutral term "man" refers only to men. Dudes that is.

check, I don't dodge it; I cash it; not for nothing am I renowned for ECONOMIC ANALYSIS OF LAW!

Several of the tweets express puzzlement at my having said in a recent oral argument concerning employment discrimination against a lesbian: "why are there lesbians?" It does sound a little like asking "why are there iguanas?" But what I meant was what is the causality of lesbianism? Is it something you choose the way you choose a dress? Or is it innate, genetic, like whether you're born male or female? I think clearly the latter.

Actually, I don't remember having said "why are there lesbians?" I thought I just asked the employer's lawyer what he thought caused some women to become lesbians. This makes me wonder how many of the quotations attributed to me in @Posner_Thoughts are authentic. Well, most of them either are or should be authentic because they are very funny and I am very funny! For example:

> MAKING EXPLODING OFFERS TO LAW CLERK APPLICANTS IS VERY WRONG. ESPECIALLY WHEN THEY HAVE AN INTERVIEW SCHEDULED WITH ME.

> ACADEMICS AND CIVIL SERVANTS ARE LAZY BUT JUDGES TAKE THE LAZINESS CAKE— USUALLY BAKED BY THEIR LAW CLERKS.

I WOULD ADVISE AGAINST ACCEPTING A CUPCAKE FROM MICHAEL DORF. HE LIKES STUFF THAT'S HALF BAKED.

I DON'T LIKE EMOTIONAL THINGS; I DO LIKE CATS.

EVERY SCHOLAR HAS HAD AN IDEA ONLY TO FIND SOMEONE ELSE HAS ALREADY WRITTEN ABOUT IT. USUALLY THE SOMEONE ELSE IS ME.

But there is at least one mistake!: I have never thought or said or written that the late JUDGE CUDAHY [WAS] A ROTTEN WRITER. *HE WAS AN EXCELLENT WRITER!*

FOREWORD

Richard A. Posner recently retired as the most prominent and outspoken jurist of his time. He sat for nearly 36 years on the United States Court of Appeals for the Seventh Circuit, but his interests and influence reach far beyond the bench. He is the author of over 40 books, more than 3300 judicial opinions, and countless articles in law journals, magazines, newspapers, and online.[1] He is more often cited by name in others' writing than any other judge, ever. He was a founder and leader of the law and economics movement, and his writings cover a wide range of topics, from terrorism to sex laws to economics to aging to privacy, the impeachment of Bill Clinton, and, of course, the merits and failings (mostly failings) of the United States federal judicial system.

Posner's improbable productivity is notable on its own, but what truly sets him apart is the breadth of his intellectual reach and the clarity (some might say stridency) of his expression. Posner's opinions—legal and otherwise—stem from and his pragmatist jurisprudence

---

[1] We use "over," "more than," and "countless" here because while these stats regularly accompany introductions to Posner, it's hard to keep up with them.

(we hesitate to say "philosophy," *see infra* p. 36): a relentlessly logical analysis that considers seemingly all there is to know that is relevant to the topic at hand—facts in particular cases, facts about the world, surveys of scientific and empirical research, economic analysis, academic literature, and whatever else the internet has to offer—to craft a sensible decision. He takes these materials to their logical end, never stopping short of where the analysis leads. He does not confine his views to what would be acceptable at cocktail parties,[2] and he is not afraid to take (indeed, he may even relish taking) controversial positions. What makes all of this fun (or infuriating, depending on your frame of reference) is that Posner's views are delivered without pretense, in a plain-spoken and conversational voice that will have you to nodding along even as your better instincts send warnings or—if you are a lawyer—your own argument is taken apart.

Unsurprisingly, Posner is not without his critics. He is criticized for failing to hew as closely to precedent as others would have it, for going "outside the record," and, essentially, for saying the things he does out loud. But Posner's critics labor under the severe handicap of not being Richard A. Posner (we all suffer from this). It would be impossible to complete an effective, comprehensive critique of Posner unless the would-be critic abandoned everything else in his life, forever, to do so. Posner's just too fast and too smart.

---

[2] He doesn't even go to cocktail parties. See *infra*, p. 10.

Enter @Posner_Thoughts (tagline: "Musings from the smartest man in the world"), an anonymous Twitter account that parodies Posner's views by reducing them to bite-size tidbits that fit within Twitter's 140-character limit. Since its launch in early 2016, @Posner_Thoughts has gathered nearly 4000 followers and its tweets have made hundreds of thousands of "impressions."[3] A testament to Posner's own popularity, followers often express delight that such an account even exists. For example:

OMG THIS ACCOUNT EXISTS

POSNER THOUGHTS @Posner_Thoughts
QUIT BABBLING. YOU'RE ANGRY AT A PARODY. twitter.com/macsva4/status...

---

[3] Statistically speaking, @Posner_Thoughts had 3924 followers as of September 9, 2017, based on 1342 tweets since Feb. 1, 2016. That amounts to about 7 new followers per day and 3 new followers per tweet. Posner_Thoughts follows 286 other Twitter users, resulting in a follow ratio over 13:1, which is very favorable according to social media marketing "experts," who advise that a 1:5 is a good follow ratio. More empirical research is sorely needed in this area, but the ratio does suggest that people follow @Posner_Thoughts out of genuine interest and not just because the account followed them first.

Posner Thoughts, *Annotated*

Twitter users have even speculated that Justice Scalia, another member of the Supreme Court (especially Kagan), or Posner himself is behind the account.[4]

What @Posner_Thoughts's followers may not realize is the extent to which the individual "thoughts" are based on specific excerpts from Posner's opinions, extrajudicial writing, and interviews. This book seeks to remedy that: With few exceptions, the "thoughts" below are followed by references to something that Posner wrote or said himself. Although "parody is always somewhat unfair"[5] we've tried to minimize the unfairness here while adhering to a high standard of amusement. Nevertheless, we admit to taking things out of context, ignoring qualifying explanations, and using some very threadbare connections for your amusement, at Posner's expense. We hope you will enjoy it and that he forgives us.

Some notes on Volume I

1. *Important!* How to use this book: Readers unfamiliar with @Posner_Thoughts on Twitter might be justifiably confused about which parts of the chapters that follow are "Posner thoughts" and which are things Posner actually said or wrote. To be clear, the "thoughts" come first. They are set in a serif font, in a larger type-

---

[4] In reverse order: not true; not true; obviously not true.
[5] As a review of Posner's ECONOMIC ANALYSIS OF THE LAW put it. See William Domnarski, RICHARD POSNER 87.

face, do not begin with quotation marks, and are not followed by a source citation in the same paragraph. The annotation—the source for each "thought"—comes in the immediately following paragraph, is longer, and is set in a smaller, sans-serif font. Annotations usually begin with quotation marks, though not always, as explained two paragraphs *infra*.

2. Sources: We're trying out Posner's suggestion to ignore the *Bluebook*, so we hope the off-the-top-of-our-heads citation style that we have employed is consistent and enables readers to readily find the cited materials if it strikes their fancy to look for them. Even so, it might be helpful to know the following: (*i*) when no author is listed, assume it is Posner; (*ii*) article titles, internet posts, and so forth are in italics; books in small caps (the title of William Domnarski's biography of Posner is RICHARD POSNER, so look out for that one); (*iii*) URLs for internet sources appear only in the bibliography because they are ugly; and (*iv*) we haven't announced short forms with parentheticals. On that last point, we hope our short forms are obvious; if not, all of our sources are in the bibliography.

3. Quotations: Where an annotation begins with a quotation, the quote is from Posner, directly or as quoted in another source. In the latter case, we trust that the quoted material is accurate, but we haven't tracked them all down (in some cases we do not have access to the original source). Nor have we always cited to the original source as the *Bluebook* would have us do. When a quotation appears parenthetically, *after* a cited source, the quotation is from the source but the words are not Posner's.

Posner Thoughts, *Annotated*

4. Oral arguments: The Seventh Circuit helpfully provides recordings of oral arguments at the following address: media.ca7.uscourts.gov/oralArguments/oar.jsp, where one can find the arguments cited below.

5. Thought fidelity: The thoughts in this book are not exactly as they first appeared on Twitter (*if* they first appeared on Twitter; many of them are new). For example, @Posner_Thoughts tweets in all capital letters. When accused of shouting, @Posner_Thoughts explains: MY THOUGHTS ARE LOUD. For this book, we have limited all caps to the chapter titles. We have also expanded some abbreviations that were employed to keep within Twitter's 140-character limit.

6. Quotation style: This book adopts some unlegalistic (if not antilegalistic) stylistic conventions for readability's sake. For example, sometimes we have deleted parts of quotations (like parentheticals) without telling you. And we're not just talking about parentheticals that follow a legal citation. Posner often includes asides and comments in his writing; sometimes they are set apart by parentheses, sometimes by dashes, and sometimes by commas. On rare occasions they appear in a footnote. While such asides are helpful in context, they can distract from pithy quotations of the sort that this book relies on.[6]

---

[6] For more information and a proposed solution to this problem in ordinary legal writing, see Jack Metzler, Cleaning Up Quotations, ssrn.com/abstract=2935374.

This doesn't mean we're just stringing unconnected words together to make up things that Posner never said. The omitted material (mostly parentheticals) is truly extraneous, such that the sentence still stands on its own without it. We've otherwise toed the line on other omissions, which, with one exception mentioned below, are indicated by ellipses.

To just drop part of a quote without even an ellipsis is anathema in a legal document—sanctionable in front of the wrong judge. But this is not a legal document. It's meant to be fun, and repeatedly reading "parenthetical omitted" or "footnote omitted," or skipping over a bunch of ellipses isn't much fun for normal people.

If you're reading this book for a non-fun reason like research, you most likely are making a grave error. If you insist on doing so against our advice, be warned that you will want to scrupulously check for missing parentheticals and footnotes before you try copying something from here and claiming it's an exact quote. And while we're confessing, if there are any "internal citations omitted," (and there are) we haven't mentioned that either. We were even considering doing away with brackets to change capitalization and so forth,[7] but that seemed like a bridge too far. We think Posner would

---

[7] The short citation guide that Posner gives his clerks permits leaving out brackets when changing upper case to lower case. THE FEDERAL JUDICIARY 63. Unfortunately, all but one of our capitalization changes were from lower case to upper case.

approve of these conventions and the reasons behind them.[8] If he doesn't, we'll probably hear about it.

> @Posner_Thoughts
> Jack Metzler
> Washington, D.C.
> September 9, 2017

---

[8] A system of citation should seek to "economize on space and the reader's time" and "minimize distraction." REFLECTIONS ON JUDGING 97.

POSNER THOUGHTS
annotated

Chapter Zero
READ ME!

Things in this book that look like this are "Posner Thoughts" (except this one). They are supposed to be funny (same).

> Things typeset like this (except this one) are things that Judge Posner actually said or wrote. They are followed by a reference to where he said or wrote that thing. For more information, check the first item under "Some notes on Volume I," *supra* p. xii.

Chapter One
CALL ME DICK*

Don't you know who I am?

"Why do you want our C.V.s at this stage? Don't you know who I am?" William Domnarski, RICHARD POSNER 147.

My mother was a tiger mom before the Asians thought of it.

"[M]y mother ... pushed me ... much as Asian American parents push their kids." REFLECTIONS ON JUDGING 18–19 n. 1.

---

* "I require my law clerks to call me by my first name." REFLECTIONS ON JUDGING 128.

My parents always called me Dick.

"But my parents always called me 'Dick.'" Ronald K.L. Collins, *The Man Behind the Robes—A Q&A with Richard Posner* (Dec. 1, 2014).

My preschool was highly regarded, and even more so once I entered.

"[T]he well-known Walden School, in Manhattan." REFLECTIONS ON JUDGING 18 n. 1.

I have fond memories of my prestigious preschool, which I entered early.

"I entered first grade earlier than most kids ... because I had started in nursery school ... at two years, eight months." REFLECTIONS ON JUDGING 18–19 n. 1.

My preschool teacher nailed it: "Dickie is in awe of his own capacities."

Domnarski 12–13 ("Dickie has matured so rapidly that he himself seems to stand a little in awe of his own capacities.").

All my life people have noted how exceptional I am. My high school classmates gave me an appropriate nickname: "the Brain."

> Domnarski 15 ("The yearbook reveals that his nickname was 'The Brain.'").

I never graduated from high school. Didn't need to.

> "I entered Yale College in 1959 at sixteen, having skipped my last year of high school." REFLECTIONS ON JUDGING 19.

I didn't so much drop *out* of high school as drop *up*, to Yale.

> "If I had remained in high school for the fourth year and reapplied then I would have been admitted [to Harvard]; but I wanted to get on with my career." REFLECTIONS ON JUDGING 19.

I was a brat of the best sort in college.

> "[A] disrespectful brat at Yale College in the 1950s." Domnarski 22.

I told my ethics professor in college that his life's work was trivial. It totally was.

> "I can well understand your annoyance at [my views], since, were they justified, they would destroy your *raison d'être* as a moral philosopher. No one likes his life's work called trivial." Domnarski 22.

I still shudder to think of the mass of mediocre undergrad minds at Yale, hostile to the truly bright student.

> "The bright student often feels isolated by the hostility of a mass of mediocre minds centered in an upperclass core." Domnarski 26.

One college professor commented: "You give the impression of being so right," which he wanted me to change. *As if.*

> Domanarski 20–21 ("You give the impression of being so right. Even if you are, you should be careful not to convey that precise impression.").

My portrayal of Renfield in Dick Cavett's staging of *Dracula* was eerily accurate.

Domnarski 23 ("Senior year he played the minor character Renfield in *Dracula*. It was directed by Dick Cavett.").

I went to Harvard Law School because Yale seemed too easy.

"I interviewed at Yale, but Harvard just seemed so much more challenging. Yale seemed so lax; it seemed to me you had to go to Harvard—go to the tough place, don't go to the easy place." Domnarski 28.

Erwin Griswold sucked as a law prof.

"My particular *bête noir* at Harvard was the Dean, Dean Griswold. Terrible teacher, terrible … unprepared and unresponsive." BookTV, *William Domnarski discusses Richard Posner*, CSPAN (Oct. 4, 2016).

I became president of Harvard Law Review based on my grades, unlike Obama, for example.

"Membership was based entirely on grades (that is no longer the case)." REFLECTIONS ON JUDGING 20.

When I was president of the Harvard Law Review, the only perks were a weekly happy hour and an annual banquet.

"In my day—if I may be permitted a moment of old fogeyism—the only perks were the banquet, held on the eve of the election of the law review president, and a Friday afternoon cocktail party for the review's officers." REFLECTIONS ON JUDGING 103 n. 103.

Back then a Supreme Court clerkship was no real biggie.

"[A] Supreme Court clerkship was not that big a deal." *The Supreme Court and Celebrity Culture*, 88 Chicago-Kent L. Rev. 299, 301 (2013).

CALL ME DICK

I never applied to clerk for Judge Friendly. Even so, he made a real mistake not hiring me.

"I did not apply for a clerkship, although, as mentioned in the previous chapter, I received one. I have long regretted not having applied for a clerkship with Judge Friendly, as I think I would have learned more than from a Supreme Court clerkship." REFLECTIONS ON JUDGING 42 n. 4.

I loved my mother very much, until I was about 20 years old anyway.

"I loved her very much when I was a child and indeed until I was about 20." Domnarski 174.

When I clerked there I thought the Supreme Court was unimpressive. It's gone downhill since then.

"I found the Supreme Court an unimpressive institution." REFLECTIONS ON JUDGING 21.

Before clerking for Justice Brennan I was impressed by his opinions—turned out the best ones were written by a former clerk. Typical.

"I read a number of his opinions and was impressed by them; only later did I learn that the best of them had been written by a former clerk of his." REFLECTIONS ON JUDGING 21.

My Supreme Court clerkship was a breeze.

"I worked less hard that year than any year since." REFLECTIONS ON JUDGING 21.

I once changed the outcome of a Supreme Court case by accident.

"I was under the mistaken impression that the Court had voted to reverse. . . . When Justice Brennan read my opinion, he said it was persuasive and he'd tried to persuade the Court to change its vote from affirm to reverse. His persuasive efforts much have been effective, though I don't recall his having said anything to me about them." Ronald K.L. Collins, *The Judge & Company – Questions for Judge Posner from Judges, Law Professors & a Journalist*, Concurring Opinions (Dec. 3, 2014) (discussing *Gray v. Sanders*, 372 U.S. 368 (1963)).

I hated the sixties then. Still do. Adele I like.

"I hated [sixties counterculture]; I still hate it."; "I like contemporary popular music a lot—Kelly Clarkson, Sara Bareilles, Taylor Swift, Adele, OneRepublic, Bruno Mars, etc." Collins, *The Man Behind the Robes*.

When I first became a law professor I thought I wouldn't do much publishing. LOL.

Domnarski 56 ("[H]e had told Bayless Manning that he didn't see himself writing academic articles.").

Breaking up AT&T, which, by the way, led to those fancy phones you all carry, was my idea.

Domnarski 52 (Posner "wrote a forty-page memorandum explaining that AT&T was violating antitrust rules on vertical integration and that the company should be broken up.").

Posner Thoughts, *Annotated*

I made some bank consulting for AT&T when the government sued to break it up.

> "So I said: sure, why not?" *The Decline and Fall of AT&T: A Personal Recollection*, 61 FCC L. J. 11, 14 (2008). "It was lucrative, it was fun, I learned a lot." *Id.* at 19.

I considered not becoming a judge because of the pay.

> "I had a large income from consulting." Howard Bashman, *20 Questions for Circuit Judge Richard A. Posner of the U.S. Court of Appeals for the Seventh Circuit*, How Appealing (Dec. 1, 2003).

I would have turned down the judgeship if it meant a real financial sacrifice.

> "I would have refused had it meant a real financial sacrifice or the job had been uninteresting." REFLECTIONS ON JUDGING 26.

When I was nominated the ABA gave me a "qualified" rather than "well qualified" rating.

Bet they feel pretty stupid now.

> "The ABA committee, unimpressed by my academic accomplishments, and negatively impressed by my lack of trial experience . . . rated me 'qualified' but not 'well qualified.'" REFLECTIONS ON JUDGING 27.

When asked an uncomfortable question during your Senate confirmation hearing, the rational choice is to lie, is what I told myself.

> "I answered Thurmond's question by saying, 'I am afraid they were not able to come with me.' (I confess I wasn't being honest.)." REFLECTIONS ON JUDGING 31.

There's no way around it: the training I received after becoming a judge blew chunks.

> "It lasted one or two days and had little content as near as I can recall. In fact all I can recall is an argument over how to designate sections and subsections of opinions, with Judge Ruggero Aldisert, who was giving a talk to the group, very insistent that they should be designated as statutory sections and subsections generally are (that is, I(a)(1)(A)(i)—I don't know what comes next)." REFLECTIONS ON JUDGING 32.

The chief judge wouldn't give me extra work during my first year as a judge. *Big mistake.*

> Domnarski 98 ("In his first year he asked the chief judge for extra work but was told no.").

I was a law school gunner and a law professor gunner, so naturally I became a judicial gunner.

> Domnarski 98 ("Posner's habit now was to write his opinions at home the evening of oral argument.").

I don't go to cocktail parties.

"I don't go to cocktail parties. I don't go to conventions or bar events—or at least very, very rarely." Joel Cohen, *An Interview With Judge Richard A. Posner*, ABA Journal (July 2014).

I slipped the title of an Adele song into an opinion once.

"Allegations based on 'information and belief' thus won't do in a fraud case—for 'on information and belief' can mean as little as 'rumor has it that . . . .'" *United States ex rel. Bogina v. Medline Indus.*, 809 F.3d 365, 370 (7th Cir. 2016).

I don't worry about being controversial. Haters gonna hate.

"I don't care about that." Cohen, *An Interview With Judge Richard A. Posner* (whether "a dust-up with Justice Scalia . . . deflects from the respect the judiciary might have in the eyes of the public, or even the bar itself").

No one has ever written so much pleasing to so few and offensive to so many.

"[N]o one has ever written so much pleasing to so few and offensive to so many." Domnarski 255.

I could fill up Twitter.

"I'm a compulsive writer." Noah Charney, *How I Write: Richard Posner*, Daily Beast (Nov. 7, 2013).

I am a monster.
All of the best minds are.

"I am a monster. . . . [T]he most interesting, creative—I would say, the most worthwhile—human beings [are] monsters like Wagner, Tolstoy, Nietzsche, Wittgenstein, Proust, Kafka, Newton, and Michelangelo, etc." Domnarski 251–252.

Chapter Two
I AM NOT A SOUR PUSS*

I am surrounded by sycophants.

"I am surrounded by sycophants." The Second Life of Judge Richard A. Posner.

I don't read popular fiction.

"I am a resolute nonreader of popular fiction, nonviewer of television, and nonmoviegoer." *The Depiction of Law in* The Bonfire of the Vanities, 98 Yale L. J. 1653, 1653 (1989).

I don't like emotional things.
I do like cats.

"I don't like emotional things. Adventure is fine, but I don't like things that are sad." Noah Charney, *How I Write: Richard Posner*, Daily Beast (Nov. 7, 2013).

---

* "I'm not just a sourpuss." *The Supreme Court and Celebrity Culture,* 88 Chicago-Kent L. Rev. 299 (2013).

Humorous fiction that I agree with is brilliant.

"The reality of constitutional decisionmaking is well summarized in—of all places—a brilliant recent law novel." *What is Obviously Wrong With the Federal Judiciary, Yet Eminently Curable Part II*, 19 Green Bag 2d 257 (2016).

I am not eager to be sent to the countryside to do farm work while wearing a dunce cap.

"I am not eager to be sent to the countryside to do farm work while wearing a dunce cap." *The State of Legal Scholarship Today: A Comment on Schlag*, 97 Geo. L. J. 845, 855 (2009).

I've always felt that if I could crawl inside of Justice Holmes I would be happy there.

"[H]e cannot crawl inside him, which is what you want in a biographer. I feel, probably unwarrentedly, that *I* can crawl inside him." William Domnarski, RICHARD POSNER 151.

None of the court's so-called amici showed up to help me move this weekend. Now I have all this extra pizza.

> "Amicus curiae briefs are for the most part a complete waste of time and a complete waste of the amici's money." Bashman, 20 Questions for Circuit Judge Richard A. Posner.

Theology is not my cup of tea, even with two lumps of God.

> "I don't like theology with God, I don't like theology without God. It's preachy, it's solemn, it's dull. It's not my cup of tea at all." Lincoln Caplan, *Rhetoric and the Law*, Harvard Magazine (Jan-Feb. 2016).

When I say strip joints tend to be tawdry, you can trust that it has been thoroughly researched.

> "Establishments that purvey erotica, live or pictorial, tend to be tawdry." *Blue Canary Corp. v. City of Milwaukee*, 251 F.3d 1121, 1124 (7th Cir. 2001).

Nude dancing is an area in which I have particular expertise.

> "[N]ude dancing (my area of particular expertise)." Domnarski 142.

Liquor and sex are an explosive combination. I mean, wow!

"Liquor and sex are an explosive combination." *Blue Canary Corp. v. City of Milwaukee*, 251 F.3d 1121, 1124 (7th Cir. 2001).

Most of my cases would be nothing in the hands of another judge.

"Most of my cases would be nothing cases in the hands of other judges." Domnarski 142.

My preferred appellate panel is me, my cat, and I.

"She is a beauty, as you can see; also very intelligent." Jerry Coyne, *Readers' cats: Pixie*, Why Evolution is True.

I never look back, especially at precedent.

"Part of the psychology of judging is that you don't look back." Joel Cohen, *An Interview With Judge Richard A. Posner*, ABA Journal (July 2014).

Deference is what judges who don't understand the case do.

"Consider what judges do when they don't understand the activity from which a case before them has arisen. They duck, bluff, weave, change the subject. The principal evasive techniques are, first, deference to lower-level decision makers." REFLECTIONS ON JUDGING 85–86.

Nobody criticizes my appellate decisions, of which there are more than 3100, by the by.

Not validly anyway.

"Criticisms of my judicial opinions are rare, even though I have written more than 3100 published opinions in my 34 years as a federal appellate judge." *What Is Obviously Wrong With the Federal Judiciary, Yet Eminently Curable Part I*, 19 Green Bag 2d 187 (2016).

If the Supreme Court might take a case where I wrote the opinion and disagree with me, I make sure to tell them what they should do on any issues that would come up then.

> "Though it may seem superfluous to consider whether the Spent Fuel Act is also unconstitutional under the supremacy clause, we shall do so in order to assist the Supreme Court should it decide to review this case and in doing so disagree with our analysis of the commerce clause issue. *Illinois v. Gen'l Electric Co.*, 683 F.2d 206, 214 (7th Cir. 1982).

I like criticism rough, like a cat's tongue. The rougher the better.

> "[W]e should insist upon challenge and criticism, the rougher the better." Domnarski 146.

Hard to explain all the citations to me without bragging.

> "I don't see how I can answer this question without seeming to brag. You really ought to ask the judges who cite me why they do so. Obviously one factor in my being cited a lot is that I write more opinions than other federal appellate judges, and it may help as well that I do write my own opinions and that I try to be clear and frank and practical, and if I am right that pragmatism is the secret story of our courts these are qualities in a judicial opinion that should appeal to other judges." Bashman, *20 Questions for Circuit Judge Richard A. Posner*.

The best citation for any given proposition is usually something I've written.

> Domnarski 112 ("He cites himself, though, more than any other judge, though not by name. . . . Only if the US Supreme Court has precedent squarely on point will he cite that court first.").

When you've written all the good articles you get to cite yourself a lot.

> Domnarski 78 ("Posner answered that he pretty much had to cite himself because he had written most of the secondary literature.").

I hope you're not surprised that I invented the cat's paw theory.

> "The state is assumed to have the whip hand by virtue of the political subdivision exemption, and if it controls a private employer's labor relations it would be futile to make the employer bargain with his workers. He would just be a cat's paw. Any real bargaining would be with the state, and it is not required to bargain." *Shager v. Upjohn Co.*, 913 F.2d 398, 405 (7th Cir. 1990).

Also invented the law school gunner.

> "I loved my first year at the Harvard Law School, in all its brutishness." REFLECTIONS ON JUDGING 20.

I pretty much came up with the idea for health warnings on cigarette packages.

So you're welcome.

> "I wrote the commission's statement promulgating and justifying a rule requiring health warnings in cigarette labeling and advertising. Although quickly preempted by Congress, the rule was the beginning of the eventually very successful regulatory efforts to curb smoking." REFLECTIONS ON JUDGING 22.

My birthday cards are a delight to read. They usually run about 125 pages.

> "I'm a compulsive writer." Charney, How I Write: Richard Posner.

Henry Friendly told me that every one of my opinions is a masterpiece. No, seriously.

> Domnarski 99 ("'Every one is a masterpiece of analysis, scholarship, and style,' he wrote.").

I AM NOT A SOUR PUSS

> Critics have sometimes called my writing "pontifical." Like it's a bad thing.

Thomas Kauper, *Review of* Antitrust Law: An Economic Perspective *by Richard Posner*, 8 Bell J. Econ. & Mgmt. Sci. 609 (1977) ("[H]is style has a pontifical quality from time to time.").

> I'm against footnotes.

Against Footnotes, 38 Journal of the American Judges Association 24–25 (2001).

> When I publish in the best known journals it's not out of arrogance. It's for the poor economists who don't have access to lesser journals.

"My work is addressed at least as much to economists as to lawyers, and economists are not able to obtain law reviews other than those published at a handful of the best-known law schools." Domnarski 76.

I don't even respond to dissents in my opinions.

* * *

Appendix to opinion: FYI, regarding the dissent: No, no, no, not true, not even, false.

> *Rowe v. Gibson*, 798 F.3d 622, 632–635 (7th Cir. 2015) (appendix to opinion).

Even a dash of jargon will ruin a good judicial pie.

> "The realist judge has a distaste for legal jargon."
> REFLECTIONS ON JUDGING 120.

"Mushy" is sometimes the best you can do with a legal opinion. Not so with a potato.

> "I don't think it's possible to generalize. I think the judge just has to balance the competing interests. I know that's mushy, but it's the best I can do." Ronald K.L. Collins, *The Judge & Company – Questions for Judge Posner from Judges, Law Professors & a Journalist*, Concurring Opinions (Dec. 3, 2014).

Plain meaning?
Can't I at least get sprinkles?

"When interpreting a statute, you're supposed to look for 'plain meaning,' and I don't know how 'plain meaning' would differ from 'meaning.' But I can't say that's the worst." Zoe Tillman, *Q&A: Judge Posner on Writing, Law School and Cat Videos*, National Law Journal (May 18, 2016).

I use retard as a verb.

"Deprivation of food and liquids would retard rather than accelerate the fulfillment of that desire." *Atkins v. City of Chicago*, 631 F.3d 823, 831 (7th Cir. 2011).

Write for the general public?
Like they care.

"It's unrealistic for judges to try to educate the general public. I don't they the general public is interested in anything about judicial opinions except who won the case." Collins, *The Judge & Company*.

Simplify, ruthlessly.

"We shall simplify ruthlessly." *Fox Valley AMC/Jeep, Inc. v. AM Credit Corp.*, 836 F.2d 366, 367 (7th Cir. 1988).

I've received the Learned Hand Medal and the Henry Friendly Medal. Who will get the Richard Posner Medal?

Domnarski 201 ("In May 2005 he received the Learned Hand Medal for Excellence in Federal Jurisprudence, . . . and in October 2005, in what must have been an interesting ceremony, Posner received, along with Ronald Dworkin, the Henry Friendly Medal.").

Not offending people is hard, and rarely worth it.

"Yet despite this [Justice Cardozo] seems never to have given serious offense. One has to be a judge to know how difficult an achievement that was." CARDOZO: A STUDY IN REPUTATION 8.

Wait. Where was I?

"But we are wandering from the point." *Avitia v. Metropolitan Club*, 49 F.3d 1219, 1232 (7th Cir. 1995).

I blame a lot but care very little.

"I am inclined to blame, but not to care." Domnarski 253.

I AM NOT A SOUR PUSS

The thing I hate most is the lack of response to my ranting. It's pretty depressing actually.

"But no; it seems I am to remain a voice crying in the wilderness. Pretty depressing." *What is Obviously Wrong II*, 19 Green Bag 2d at 268.

* * *

I don't fear death.

I do worry what will become of the federal judiciary without me.

"As long as my physical health holds up and senility holds off, I will continue to work as I have. I am one of those people who dread retirement. I hope I won't overstay my welcome." Domnarski 246.

Chapter Three
THE POZE KNOWS*

Justice is blind but I have Google.

"So, I look for the answers, often by an Internet search." Ronald K.L. Collins, The Judge & Company – Questions for Judge Posner from Judges, Law Professors & a Journalist, Concurring Opinions (Dec. 3, 2014).

Not knowing everything is annoying. I'm trying to make sure it doesn't happen to me.

"[O]ften indeed we judges don't have enough knowledge to decide a case in a well-informed way just based on what the lawyers and the lower court or agency and doctrine tell us." Collins, *The Judge & Company*.

---

* William Domnarski, RICHARD POSNER 17 ("He coined the phrase 'the Poze knows.'").

I'm going to read the entire internet tonight.

"Google gives you access to 40 million websites, and obviously the amount of information is vast. Now it's not all information. In fact, the largest category of websites are cat videos. But still, there are only 2 million cat videos. So that leaves 38 million websites. Not all of which, but many of which, contain information. It's very useful and lucid and so on." Zoe Tillman, *Q&A: Judge Posner on Writing, Law School and Cat Videos*, National Law Journal (May 18, 2016).

The number of Google hits on a phrase is meaningful information.

"I think the number of Google hits on a word or phrase can fairly be regarded as incontestable." REFLECTIONS ON JUDGING 136.

posner performance enhancing drugs
All   News   Shopping   Images   Videos   More ▼   Search tools
About 82,100 results (0.34 seconds)

Using Google sometimes means advocates have no chance to respond.

OTOH: ¯_(ツ)_/¯

"I do need to acknowledge however reluctantly the awkwardness of judicial reliance on 'independent judicial research' (primarily Internet research by the judge or judges) at the appellate level. . . . Where the lawyers are onstage only for the time it takes . . . for oral argument, [and] rebuttal would require either reargument or supplementary briefs and either procedure could delay the decision of the appeal significantly. I don't have a solution for this problem." *What is Obviously Wrong With The Federal Judiciary, Yet Eminently Curable Part II*, 19 Green Bag 2d 257, 263 (2016).

On the internet, nobody knows you're not a raccoon.

"Anonymity is a good example of the problem. It protects but it can also be used to deceive. It is hiding the true appearance of the raccoon from me." *The Second Life of Judge Richard A. Posner.*

The best way to learn about the young is to carefully observe law clerks.

"Judging from my law clerks, young lawyers are increasingly likely to have strong backgrounds in science and technology." Collins, *The Judge & Company.*

Homosexuals should be allowed to marry, just like Eskimos.

"Although I knew in the 1950s that there were homosexuals, if asked I would have truthfully said that as far as I knew I had never met one, or expected ever to meet one, any more than I had ever met or expected to meet an Eskimo." *Homosexual Marriage*, Becker-Posner Blog (May 13, 2012).

Few men are interested in lesbians.

"Few men are interested in lesbians." *Douglass v. Hustler Magazine*, 769 F.2d 1128 (7th Cir. 1985).

Some people say stupid things in conversation just to try out their ideas. Much better to write a book first.

"Some people say stupid things because they use conversation to try out their ideas." Domnarski 195.

Some nonsense, while still nonsense, is harmless nonsense.

"But the instruction, although nonsense, was harmless nonsense." *Avitia v. Metropolitan Club*, 49 F.3d 1219, 1225 (7th Cir. 1995).

Privacy is overrated.

Privacy is overrated, N.Y. Daily News (April 28, 2013).

Brontosauruses are real.

"The Court is to the entire judiciary as the brontosaurus's brain is to its entire body." REFLECTIONS ON JUDGING 38.

Loosey and goosey are equally bad. Together they are intolerable.

"That's the basis of *lex loci delicti*, which continues to be a sound doctrine that has largely survived modern loosey-goosey conflicts doctrine." Collins, *The Judge & Company*.

Maine Coon cats are half raccoon until the Supreme Court says otherwise, no matter what Wikipedia says.

"I have a Maine Coon cat—half raccoon. Her name is Dinah. She was in the New Yorker." *The Second Life of Judge Richard A. Posner*.

One would think that nothing is more harmless to use than a knife or razor. One would be very very wrong.

"But nothing is more common or, we should have thought, more harmless than to use a knife or a razor." *Welge v. Planters Lifesavers Co.*, 17 F.3d 209, 210 (1994).

Stabbing a poodle doesn't take much time, Pixie assures me.

"Nor would it take long to stab a small poodle twice." *Bradford v. Brown*, 831 F.3d 902, 906 (7th Cir. 2016).

A Persian cat with its fur shaved is alarmingly pale and thin. Trust me on this.

"[A] Persian cat with its fur shave[d] is alarmingly pale and thin." *Schurz Communs. v. FCC*, 982 F.2d 1043, 1050 (7th Cir. 1992).

An Exacto knife is basically a razor blade with a handle. Empirically speaking, it's not good for shaving 100% of the time. Very painful.

> "Godfrey needed proof of her purchase of the jar of peanuts; so, using an Exacto knife (basically a razor blade with a handle), she removed the part of the label that contained the bar code." *Welge v. Planters Lifesavers Co.*, 17 F.3d 209 (1994).

Weeds are ambiguous.

> "But there is an ambiguity in the concept of a 'weed.'" *Discount Inn, Inc. v. City of Chicago*, 803 F.3d 317, 321 (7th Cir. 2015).

The old adage is true: a prosecutor can get a grand jury to indict a ham taco.

> "A sandwich does not have to have two slices of bread; it can have more than two (a club sandwich) and it can have just one (an open-faced sandwich). The slices of bread do not have to be thin, and the layer between them does not have to be thin either. The slices do not have to be slices of bread: a hamburger is regarded as a sandwich, and also a hot dog—and some people regard tacos and burritos as sandwiches, and a quesadilla is even more sandwich-like." *The Incoherence of Antonin Scalia*, New Republic (Aug. 24, 2012).

Appellate judges should avoid vituperative personal abuse of their brethren. District courts, ALJs, and immigration judges are another matter.

> Judges "should strive to . . . avoid what can only be interpreted as vituperative personal abuse of a colleague." Domnarski 158.

Don't be snide, I tell new judges, to other judges, anyway.

> "New Judges should be warned against dissenting at the drop of a hat, and against bluster, exaggeration, anger, and snideness directed toward their colleagues whether in person or in opinions." REFLECTIONS ON JUDGING 35.

Philosophy is stupid.

> "I don't see much role for a philosopher in the public realm." Domnarski 193.

The list of acknowledgments in a book will tell you who really wrote it.

> "[I]n the front of the book there are acknowledgments of assistance from more than 90 people, including a number of law students. My guess is that much of the book was written by research assistants and was not adequately checked." Joel Cohen, *An Interview With Judge Richard A. Posner*, ABA Journal (July 2014).

Ethics is worthless.

"I deny your easy assumption of ethics' worth." Domnarski 22.

Adele makes me question my view that most brilliant artists are psychologically disturbed.

"[B]rilliant creative people in the arts and humanities tend to be psychologically disturbed people with a few highly developed, esoteric, invisible, and impacted artistic skills." *Judicial Biography*, 70 N.Y.U. L. Rev. 502, 507 (1995).

Chapter Four
STOP BABBLING*

Let's start with what didn't please the court: your lousy brief.

"[T]he average quality of briefs is pretty low." Howard Bashman, *20 Questions for Circuit Judge Richard A. Posner of the U.S. Court of Appeals for the Seventh Circuit*, How Appealing (Dec. 1, 2003).

Spoon-feed me background facts.

"Many lawyers . . . are fearful that judges will feel insulted to be spoon-fed appropriately simplified descriptions of the technological background to a case. I can assure the reader that we will not be." REFLECTIONS ON JUDGING 93.

---

* *University of Notre Dame v. Sebelius* (Oral argument Feb. 12, 2014).

So you don't give me a Google map of the defendant's home or the sex offenders in his neighborhood, and I'm just supposed to ignore that?

> "All too often, facts that are important to a sensible decision are missing from the briefs, and indeed from the judicial record." REFLECTIONS ON JUDGING 131.

I understand your argument, but Google says otherwise.

> "But there is no evidence of that; and the City's layout (the City is the irregularly shaped area in the middle of the Google map of Oak Forest below) suggests the improbability of a racial motive for the rezoning." *Parvati Corp. v. City of Oak Forest*, 709 F.3d 678, 682 (7th Cir. 2013).

Don't serve me up a muddle and expect me to find reversible error for you, even if it's obvious what you should have argued.

> "But we cannot have a rule that in a sympathetic case an appellant can serve us up a muddle in the hope that we or our law clerks will find somewhere in it a reversible error." *Hartmann v. Prudential Ins. Co. of Am.*, 9 F.3d 1207, 1214 (7th Cir. 1993).

Thanksgiving is coming, but that doesn't mean you can put gobbledygook in your brief.

> "In addition, the plaintiffs' briefs are replete with misrepresentations; with syntactical, grammatical, and lexical errors; and with much sheer gobbledygook. The case for sanctions under Fed. R. App. P. 38 is plain." *Fox Valley AMC/Jeep, Inc. v. AM Credit Corp.*, 836 F.2d 366, 368 (7th Cir. 1988).

You can take your narrow tailoring to the haberdashery. We're talking about the law here.

> "Here's one I really dislike: 'narrow tailoring.' Isn't it funny? It means, well, you don't want to have a broad shoulder on your jacket, you want narrow tailoring." Zoe Tillman, *Q&A: Judge Posner on Writing, Law School and Cat Videos*, National Law Journal (May 18, 2016).

If you think shoveling precedent at me is going to work you've got another thing coming.

> "And so the second-biggest mistake that appellate advocates make . . . is to think they can win by rubbing the judges' noses in the precedents." How Judges Think 220.

If you try a case before me, you get one word per objection. I do this for the jury's sake. Pay no mind to my smirk.

> To "mak[e] trials more intelligible to jurors, [I] requir[e] lawyers to limit their objections to one word (so as not to distract the jury with legal mumbo-jumbo)." *What Is Obviously Wrong With the Federal Judiciary, Yet Eminently Curable Part I*, 19 Green Bag 2d 187, 189 (2016).

There are forms of coercive interrogation that go beyond simple questioning but are not torture. Oral argument comes to mind.

> "There are forms of coercive interrogation intermediate between simple questioning and torture, such as the old 'third degree,' bright light, noise. Any beating, shaking, etc. would cross the line into torture. The intermediate forms may be permissible in extreme circumstances, but not to produce evidence that could be used in court." *The Second Life of Judge Richard A. Posner*.

Oral argument tip: If you make an absurd argument I will tell you it's absurd.

> "I regard it as absurd." *Baskin v. Bogan* (Oral argument Aug. 26, 2014).

Be prepared, or be prepared to hear about not being prepared.

"One final point . . . counsel should come to an oral argument in this court prepared to supply all information material to our consideration of the appeal." *United States v. Herrera-Medina*, 853 F.2d 564, 567 (7th Cir. 1988).

To do well at oral argument, practice on a cat.

Domnarski 49 ("Posner admitted that he practice his oral arguments to his cat—to what response he did not say.").

What am I thinking right now?

"They should have known! They should have realized it was a loose end that one or more of the judges might want tied up." REFLECTIONS ON JUDGING 138.

Inquiry notice eh? Look, when we say "actual knowledge," we mean "actual knowledge."

"We have held, moreover, that 'actual knowledge' in section 1113 means actual knowledge; it does not also mean constructive knowledge, or inquiry notice." *Wolin v. Smith Barney Inc.*, 83 F.3d 847, 853 (7th Cir. 1996).

There are three judges on this panel. Pay no attention to the other two.

"A judge should be aggressive at oral argument."
REFLECTIONS ON JUDGING 129.

If I yell at you at oral argument, blame the dolt next to me for failing to understand what I'm secretly telling him with my questions.

"And tendentious questioning—questioning that indicates how the judge is leaning with regard to the merits of the appeal—is an important method of communication with the other judges on the panel." REFLECTIONS ON JUDGING 129.

When it comes to oral argument, I want to be the torturer rather than the victim.

"I want to be the torturer rather than the victim."
REFLECTIONS ON JUDGING 25.

Very clever of you to use a baldness example with this particular panel. Did you just come up with that?

"At argument Mrs. Colby's lawyer, staring fixedly at the members of this panel, likened the head of household rule to a rule disqualifying bald persons." *Colby v. J.C. Penney Co.*, 811 F.2d 1119, 1122 (7th Cir. 1987).

Nice concession! Good boy!

"At the oral argument of the appeal the plaintiff's counsel conceded with a frankness as refreshing as it is commendable . . ." *Autotrol Corp. v. Cont'l Water Sys. Corp.*, 918 F.2d 689, 695 (7th Cir. 1990).

Oral advocates, like dogs and dog people, are too eager to please.

"Dogs are servile." BookTV, *William Domnarski discusses Richard Posner*, CSPAN (Oct. 4, 2016).

You're lucky to have me on the panel to ask about stuff you left out of the brief.

"He was lucky that he was asked that question. He would not have needed luck had he included a photograph in his brief. . . . But again, he was lucky that he was asked to explain his case, and he would not have needed luck." *Effective Appellate Brief Writing*, Litigation News (Spring 2010).

If I force you to make a concession I won't hold you to it. Usually.

"But we hesitate to bind parties by concessions made in the heat of oral argument, and shall not do so here." *In re Hoskins*, 102 F.3d 311 (1996).

I'm going to interrupt you, so you're just going to have to be patient.

"I'm going to interrupt you, so you're just going to have to be patient." *Baskin v. Bogan* (Oral argument Aug. 26, 2014).

If you don't cooperate with me, I'm not going to let you continue your argument.

"[I]f you don't cooperate with me, I'm not going to let you continue your argument." *University of Notre Dame v. Sebelius* (Oral argument Feb. 12, 2014).

You have to have something better.

"You have to have something better." *Wolf v. Walker* (Oral argument Aug. 26, 2014).

Yes, I see the red light. You're not getting off that easily.

"I used to tell them peevishly that I would not have asked the question had I not wanted it answered. Failing to break their habit (it is *so* hard to change lawyer's habits), I gave up and now answer their question with "yes" or "please." REFLECTIONS ON JUDGING 109 n. .

We generally decline to supplement the record on appeal. Sometimes we make exceptions; sometimes I just Google it myself.

> "We can't begin to understand why, rather than sit back waiting for a hearing that never happened, the lawyer didn't use the documents to help support his client's motion to reduce sentence." *United States v. Miller*, 832 F.3d 703, 705 (7th Cir. 2016).

Not really in the mood for plain meaning. Think I'll go for something spicier.

> "[T]he obsessive invocation of 'plain meaning,' which is to say text devoid of real-world context." REFLECTIONS ON JUDGING 87.

No expert testimony? Don't worry, I'll tell you what an expert would have said.

> "Had an expert been appointed, the expert would have confirmed Rowe's factual representations, and would have supported Rowe's objection that the defendant lacks personal knowledges about the condition(s) Rowe had." *Rowe v. Gibson*, 798 F.3d 622 (7th Cir. 2015).

We could come up with a standard here. But you're going to lose no matter what so forget it.

"But there is no need to fix on a precise standard in this case, for under any standard Muhammad must lose." *Azeez v. Fairman*, 795 F.2d 1296, 1300 (7th Cir. 1986).

We're not going to decide an issue just because both sides want us to. Sheesh!

"The parties' desire to have us resolve an issue that is not within our power to decide troubles us deeply." *Azeez v. Fairman*, 795 F.2d 1296, 1297 (7th Cir. 1986).

I'm not taking judicial notice. I'm just saying you lose because of stuff on the internet.

"We are not deeming the Internet evidence cited in this opinion conclusive or even certifying it as being probably correct, though it may well be correct since it is drawn from reputable medical websites. We use it only to underscore the existence of a genuine dispute of material fact. . . . As we've explained, we are not invoking Fed. R. Evid. 201 and thus not taking judicial notice of any facts outside the district court record." *Rowe v. Gibson*, 798 F.3d 622, 629, 631 (7th Cir. 2015).

Reverse trademark confusion — are you *trying* to lose?

"But here we have the converse case of 'reverse passing off,' in which the plaintiff complains that the defendant is trying to pass off the plaintiff's product as the defendant's. Why would anyone want to do such a thing?" *Peaceable Planet, Inc. v. Ty, Inc.*, 362 F.3d 986, 987 (7th Cir. 2004).

What the—? This is a prisoner case over 39 bucks FFS.

"We cannot forbear to express concern about the waste of judicial resources that is involved in allowing a person to obtain two levels of federal judicial review of an agency's denial of a claim for $ 39.20." *Savage v. CIA*, 826 F.2d 561 (7th Cir. 1987).

And by the way, district court I'm reversing: Appoint an expert and make the defendants pay for it. We clear?

"We urge the district court judge to give serious consideration to recruiting a lawyer to represent Rowe; appointing a neutral expert witness . . .; or doing both . . . [and] to order the defendants to pay the expert a reasonable fee if the expert is unwilling to work for nothing." *Rowe v. Gibson*, 798 F.3d 622, 631–632 (7th Cir. 2015).

Don't take that tone with me, district court.

"Because of the abruptness and irregularity of the district judge's handling of this case, and the unmistakable tone of derision that pervades his opinion, we have decided that further proceedings in the district court should be before a different district judge." *Stuart v. Local 727, Int'l Brotherhood of Teamsters*, 771 F.3d 1014, 1020 (7th Cir. 2014).

When I reverse it's not because I don't like you. It's because you're stupid.

"[H]ow one regards the judge's ability will, in a close case, have an influence. But I don't think any of us would react adversely to a district judge who happened not to like us." Joel Cohen, *An Interview With Judge Richard A. Posner*, ABA Journal (July 2014).

Circuit rule 36 shall apply on remand.

(That means the case is reassigned because you blew it bad, district court.)

"Circuit rule 36 shall apply on remand." *Del Raine v. Carlson*, 826 F.2d 698, 705 (7th Cir. 1987); 7th Cir. R. 36 ("Reassignment of remanded cases").

Remand for trial? What a waste of time.

> "[O]rdering a remand would be a waste of time." *Door Sys. v. Pro-Line Door Sys.*, 83 F.3d 169, 174 (7th Cir. 1996).

Chapter Five
HELL IS OTHER JUDGES

Good morning fellow panel members. You'll be pleased to know that I'll be taking the hard cases off your hands again. You're welcome.

> "[M]ost of the time, we're sitting in panels of three judges, so we split up the case among three judges. Sometimes I assign myself a little more than a third, because I'm selfish." Noah Charney, *How I Write: Richard Posner*, Daily Beast (Nov. 7, 2013).

Also, if you have any questions for the advocates, please wait until I've asked the important things.

> "A judge should be aggressive at oral argument." REFLECTIONS ON JUDGING 129.

Let me tell you about federal judges:

> HOW JUDGES THINK; THE BEHAVIOR OF FEDERAL JUDGES.

Judges don't know enough to be sensible.

"[W]e judges often don't know enough about a case to decide it sensibly, because often all we know is what the lawyers tell us, which is often very little. And when we don't have enough knowledge to decide a case in an informed way, we necessarily fall back on how we 'feel' about the case." Joel Cohen, *An Interview With Judge Richard A. Posner*, ABA Journal (July 2014).

I know how judges think, and it's not pretty.

HOW JUDGES THINK.

Federal judges' chambers are like Vegas: what happens there stays there.

"'[W]hat goes on in chambers stays in chambers' is the rule in almost all judges' offices, though not in mine." *What is Obviously Wrong II*, at 263.

Judges do some wild things.

"This is not to say that judges don't do some wild things." *The Depiction of Law in* The Bonfire of the Vanities, 98 Yale L. J. 1653, 1659 n. 5 (1989).

If you play poker with a judge, remember that they are great bluffers.

> "Judges are great bluffers, and it is particularly difficult for nonlawyers to penetrate the bluff unless they are highly cynical." *Judicial Biography*, 70 N.Y.U. L. Rev. 502, 514 (1995).

They party like rock stars at the Supreme Court.

> "The Justices joke and clown, interrupt each other, give the impression of playing to the crowd—and certainly seem to be having a good time." THE BEHAVIOR OF FEDERAL JUDGES 314.

Judges are not sending their best opinions. They're sending opinions with a lot of problems, inauthentic, overlong, formalistic. They're drafted by clerks. And some, I assume, are good lawyers.

> "But I also think that clerk-written opinions tend to be inauthentic, dull, overlong, and excessively formalistic." Ronald K.L. Collins, *The Judge & Company – Questions for Judge Posner from Judges, Law Professors & a Journalist*, Concurring Opinions (Dec. 3, 2014).

Talking to judges at conference is awkward; better to communicate by berating oral advocates.

"[Q]uestioning that indicates how the judge is leaning with regard to the merits of the appea[l] is an important method of communication with the other judges on the panel. The deliberations that follow oral argument often are stilted." REFLECTIONS ON JUDGING 129.

Judges are petty. But that's not their biggest problem.

"But I don't think petty reactions of judges to other judges or to litigants or their lawyers is a serious problem." Cohen, *An Interview With Judge Richard A. Posner.*

Half of the federal bench would resign if they had to write their own opinions.

"Half of them would resign immediately [if forced to write their own opinions]." BookTV, *William Domnarski discusses Richard Posner*, CSPAN (Oct. 4, 2016).

Academics and civil servants are lazy, but judges take the laziness cake — baked by their law clerks.

> "There's a work-ethic problem for some judges — you always have that when you have tenure; you have it with academics, with civil servants. But the most secure tenure is that of a federal judge." Cohen, *An Interview With Judge Richard A. Posner*.

After my law clerks and I debate upcoming cases, we read other chambers' bench memos and LOL.

> Domnarski 97 ("After the cases had been discussed, Posner and his clerks would read the bench memos that had been produced from the other chambers.").

Judges don't understand grammar, and it shows.

> "I think opinions have become longer, more formalistic, and more uniform, also less colorful and less individual, as a result of the near-universal delegation of opinion writing to law clerks. The steady decline in the literary culture in America, and of knowledge of grammar, also show." Collins, *The Judge & Company*.

You have to look at the briefs to see how much the judge stole from them in the opinion.

> "No evaluative study of an individual judge is complete until his opinions are compared with the lawyers' briefs. . . . [A]n attempt must be made to separate the judge's work from that of his ghosts." *Judicial Biography*, 70 N.Y.U. L. Rev. 502, 522 (2013).

If judges can't be eloquent (they can't) they should at least try to be clear.

> "No judge or Justice today writes eloquently, as Holmes and Hand and Brandeis and Cardozo and Jackson and a few others once did. . . . Clarity, not eloquence, is the only attainable though not attained, literary goal of modern judicial writing." *What Is Obviously Wrong With the Federal Judiciary, Yet Eminently Curable Part I*, 19 Green Bag 2d 187, 197 (2016).

Most judicial opinions huff and they puff, but the analysis rarely blows the house down.

> "At long last, after much huffing and puffing, comes the analysis in the opinion, often well concealed in quotations from previous judicial opinions, in bromides that do not describe actual judicial practice, in strings of citations that would be seen not to support the decision if anyone bothered to read the cited cases, and in vacuous appeals to 'plain meaning' or made-up legislative 'intent.'" REFLECTIONS ON JUDGING 251.

"For the foregoing reasons"? Give me a break.

> "Were 'for the foregoing reasons' deleted, would the reader think that the judge was concealing the reasons for the decision?" *What Is Obviously Wrong I*, 19 Green Bag 2d at 194.

It would be nice to see a well-written opinion by *someone else* once in a while.

> "I admire witty and concise opinions, remembering Holmes' adage that a judge doesn't have to be heavy in order to be weighty." *Alliance to End Repression v. Chicago*, 733 F.2d 1187, 1193 (7th Cir. 1984).

A judge who says he's not influenced by anything outside the record is lying or fooling himself.

> "Many judges would say that nothing outside 'the law,' in the narrow sense that confines the word to the texts of formal legal documents, influences *their* judicial votes at all. Some of them are speaking for public consumption, and know better. Those who are speaking sincerely are fooling themselves." REFLECTIONS ON JUDGING 130.

Sometimes appellate judges just guess.

> "A fourth tactic that judges employ to avoid having to wrestle with complex cases is to wing it, substituting a guess for data." REFLECTIONS ON JUDGING 88.

I witheringly dissent.

"I want to note finally my disquiet at the statement in the majority opinion that 'district judges may set their own sentencing policy.' . . . The result of such deference is bound to be arbitrariness in sentencing. Defendants deserve better." *United States v. Carson*, 821 F.3d 849, 855 (7th Cir. 2016) (dissenting, obviously).

Judges are not competent historians.

"Judges are not competent historians." *The Incoherence of Antonin Scalia*, New Republic (Aug. 24, 2012).

Judges criticize the political mote in the legislative and executive branches' eye, ignoring the political plank in their own.

"And so it is self-servingly silly for judges to refer to Congress and the President as 'the political branches' of the federal government, in supposed contrast to the judiciary conceived of as 'apolitical.'" *What is Obviously Wrong With The Federal Judiciary, Yet Eminently Curable Part II*, 19 Green Bag 2d 257, 264–265 (2016).

A judge who says he "respectfully dissents" is definitely lying.

An "insincere verbal curts[y]." REFLECTIONS ON JUDGING 250.

Note to noob judges: don't rely on the fake news sites. Better yet, leave the internet to me.

> "A realist judge's law clerks should Google the parties and do other online research to help them and their judge understand the parties, the commercial or scientific or other context of the case, and the activities of the parties or others that gave rise to the case." REFLECTIONS ON JUDGING 127.

Slink away, dissenting dogs.

> "And speaking of dissenters: Would they have had the courage of their convictions had they been able to pick up a fifth vote? Or would they have been like the dog that barks ferociously when it's behind a fence, but open the gate and it slinks away timidly?" *Supreme Court Year in Review: Chief Justice Roberts did the right thing—but it's still a bad law*, Slate (June 29, 2012).

Magistrate judges? Hello?

> "The magistrate remarked, delphically, that 'it also appears that principles of qualified immunity would bar some of plaintiff's claims against certain defendants.' Which claims? Which defendants? We are not told." *Del Raine v. Carlson*, 826 F.2d 698, 707 (7th Cir. 1987).

Magistrate judges are barely even judges.

"The term 'magistrate,' often used in place of 'judge' to designate the judicial officer who issues warrants, is an acknowledgment that warrants usually are issued by the most junior judicial officers." *United States v. Dessart*, 823 F.3d 395 , 406 (7th Cir. 2016) (concurring opinion).

It really chapped my horn when they started calling magistrates and bankruptcy referees "judges."

"The thirst for prestige is manifested primarily in opposition to any large increase in the number of judges, at least high-level judges, and to extending the title 'judge' to lower-level judicial personnel, such as magistrates and bankruptcy referees (now called 'magistrate judges' and 'bankruptcy judges,' to the dismay of many Article III judges)." OVERCOMING LAW 118.

The magistrate judge's analysis was not adequate. As usual.

"The magistrate's analysis was not adequate, and therefore his determination cannot stand." *Del Raine v. Carlson*, 826 F.2d 698, 705 (7th Cir. 1987).

And administrative law judges. FFS.

"The administrative law judge's decision was unreasoned, and should not have been affirmed." *Cole v. Colvin*, 831 F.3d 411 (7th Cir. 2016).

ALJs are the chicken deboners of the judicial process.

"If he is a worker on a poultry processing assembly line and the conveyor belt that carries the chickens to his work station for deboning is speeded up, he will spend less time deboning each chicken than he might think desirable to make sure no bits of bone are left in the chicken when it leaves his work station on the conveyor belt. . . . His situation would parallel that of the administrative law judges." *Association of Administrative Law Judges v. Colvin*, 777 F.3d 402, 405 (7th Cir. 2015).

ALJs would be able to handle 500 cases a year if they worked hard enough.

"What's the evidence in this case that the judges can't work harder and handle 500 cases?" *Association of Administrative Law Judges v. Colvin*, 777 F.3d 402 (7th Cir. 2015) (Oral argument Dec. 9, 2014).

This ALJ thinks watching TV proves you have a long attention span. Good grief.

"[W]e expressed skepticism about an administrative law judge's assertion that 'ability to watch television for several hours indicates a long attention span.'" *Voigt v. Colvin*, 781 F.3d 871, 878 (7th Cir. 2015).

The only judges worse than ALJs are immigration judges.

"It is one more indication of systemic failure by the judicial officers of the immigration service to provide reasoned analysis for the denial of applications for asylum." William Domnarski, RICHARD POSNER 208.

The average immigration "judge" is less qualified for the job than the average furry Maine Coon.

"[T]hese administrative law judges are overworked and many—especially the immigration judges—appear to be underqualified." REFLECTIONS ON JUDGING 94.

This immigration judge thinks sex with women disproves bisexuality. I can't even.

"Apparently the immigration judge does not know the meaning of *bisexual*." *Fuller v. Lynch*, 833 F.3d 866, 874 (7th Cir. 2016) (dissenting opinion).

It hurts to call them "judges."

"Immigration judges, by the way, though called 'judges,' are not judges in the sense that Supreme Court Justices, federal court of appeals judges, and federal district judges are." REFLECTIONS ON JUDGING 67.

Chapter Six
THE SUPREME COURT IS AWFUL[*]

I don't like the Supreme Court.

"Well, I don't like the Supreme Court." Noah Charney, *How I Write: Richard Posner*, Daily Beast (Nov. 7, 2013).

The court is at a real nadir.

"I think it's reached a real nadir." BookTV, *William Domnarski discusses Richard Posner*.

It's not even a real court.

"I don't think it's a real court." Charney, *How I Write: Richard Posner*.

---

[*] "The Supreme Court is awful." BookTV, *William Domnarski discusses Richard Posner*, CSPAN (Oct. 4, 2016).

The Justices are not super.

"They are competent. But are they super? No, because quality is only one of the criteria that Presidents and Senators consider." *What is Obviously Wrong With The Federal Judiciary, Yet Eminently Curable Part II*, 19 Green Bag 2d 257, 267 (2016).

Justices don't come smart like they used to.

"I don't think the Court at present has incandescent intellects of the caliber of Holmes, Louis Brandeis, Jackson, and Frankfurter." Eric Segall, *Judge Richard Posner, U.S. Court of Appeals for the Seventh Circuit*, New York Review of Books 47, 48 (Sept. 29, 2011).

Few, if any, of the current Justices would have been accepted at my preschool.

"[T]he well-known Walden School, in Manhattan." REFLECTIONS ON JUDGING 18 n. 1.

All but one of the Supreme Court Justices are culturally stunted.

"Among the current Supreme Court Justices, only Justice Breyer appears to have genuine cultural depth." *What Is Obviously Wrong With the Federal Judiciary, Yet Eminently Curable Part I*, 19 Green Bag 2d 187, 197 (2016).

I do not doubt that the Justices did graduate from law school (not that it shows).

"This could be misunderstood to mean that I think the others lack the necessary paper credentials, of which the most important are graduating from a law school and passing the bar exam (though one of our greatest Justices, Robert Jackson, had just a year of law school, and did not graduate). That was not my intention in using the word 'qualified' (if I did use it). I meant good enough to be a Supreme Court Justice." Above the Law, *Judge Richard Posner Corrects The Record Regarding His Supreme Court Comments* (Oct. 28, 2016).

Most—but not all—of the Justices don't even know how to sext.

"Transcripts of oral arguments before the Court reveal misunderstandings, by a number of Justices, of the elementary technology of pagers, text messaging, on-line searching, Internet service, providers, V-chips, voicemail, and the Kindle reader." REFLECTIONS ON JUDGING 79.

John Roberts is a terrible manager.

"I don't think it's well managed and I don't think the Justices are doing a good job." Above the Law, *Judge Richard Posner Corrects The Record*.

What kind of manager lets the Court take five years to publish its decisions?

> "It takes them five years to publish their opinions in the U.S. Reports. That gives them five years to tinker with the opinions before they become final." First Amendment Salon (May 16, 2016).

He's a big phony.

> "He says a lot of things that are completely phony." First Amendment Salon (May 16, 2016).

That whole "balls and strikes" thing made me throw up in my mouth a little bit.

> "If confirmation hearings were serious inquiries into a candidate's fitness rather than a low form of political theater, Roberts's statement would have been disqualifying." REFLECTIONS ON JUDGING 110–111 n. 2.

By the way, when I slam the Supreme Court, Scalia is included. He can't escape by dying.

> "I sometimes ask myself: whether the nine current Supreme Court Justices (I'm restoring Scalia to life for this purpose) are the nine best-qualified lawyers to be Justices. Obviously not." Above the Law, *Judge Richard Posner Corrects The Record.*

My cat has impeccable taste.

She disliked Scalia.

> "There is no personal animosity between Justice Scalia and me, or at least not on my side." Above the Law, *The Benchslap Dispatches: Posner v. Scalia — Is It Personal?* (Sept. 5, 2012).

Unlike Scalia, I think it's okay to consider whether a decision will cause hundreds of deaths. But that's just me.

> "I don't' agree with Justice Scalia that indifference to hundreds of deaths that might result from the Supreme Court's embracing a broad interpretation of the Second Amendment is the sign of a good judge." REFLECTIONS ON JUDGING 121.

Scalia was excitable and prone to anger.

> "He's excitable and prone to anger." Joel Cohen, *An Interview With Judge Richard A. Posner*, ABA Journal (July 2014).

Pixie thinks it's okay to dance on Scalia's grave now. I'm still waiting, mostly.

> "I regard the posthumous encomia for Scalia as absurd." *Supreme Court Breakfast Table: The academy is out of its depth*, Slate (June 24, 2016).

Justice Alito doesn't make sense.

"Alito says that states that want to prohibit same-sex marriage 'worry that by officially abandoning the older understanding, they may contribute to marriage's further decay.' This doesn't make sense." *Supreme Court Breakfast Table: The chief justice's dissent is heartless*, Slate (June 27, 2015).

I'm not sure that Alito can even count.

"He deplores the fact that 'a bare majority of Justices can invent a new right and impose that right on the rest of the country.' Would he be content had the vote been 6–3 rather than 5–4? I doubt it." *Supreme Court Breakfast Table: The chief justice's dissent is heartless.*

On the other hand, Alito did call me "the smartest man in the world."

Pearson v. Callahan, 555 U.S. 223 (2009) (Oral argument Oct. 6, 2009) ("Judge Posner . . . he's the smartest man in the world. He knows everything there is to know about law and economics and jurisprudence and literature and many other subjects.").

I have no problem with Sotomayor judging a dispute on Sesame Street, even though obviously no jurisdiction.

> "And just to show that I'm not just a sourpuss, I have no criticism of Justice Sotomayor's appearance on Sesame Street adjudicating a dispute between two stuffed animals. . . . There was no pretense that she was engaged in a serious intellectual activity." *The Supreme Court and Celebrity Culture*, 88 Chicago-Kent L. Rev. 299 (2013).

Justice Kagan says she misses Scalia. OK Elena!

> "[A]n effusive, *very* hard-to-believe, recent statement by Justice Kagan . . . 'I just loved Justice Scalia, and I miss him every day' (could that be tongue in cheek?)." *Michael C. Dorf's "Review" of Richard A. Posner*, Divergent Paths: The Academy and the Judiciary, 166 J. Legal Ed. 203, 207 (2016).

This whole certiorari business is unseemly.

> "And they decide which cases to hear, which doesn't strike me as something judges should do." Charney, *How I Write: Richard Posner*.

The Justices grant fewer cases so they have time for book tours and interviews with sycophants.

> "I don't think the lightening of the Court's caseload is the only reason for the Justices' increased immersion in the modern celebrity culture, but it is a reason." REFLECTIONS ON JUDGING 46.

The Supreme Court has mastered the art of doing less with more.

> "[D]espite the large quality-adjusted increase in the Court's staff, the Court's output has decreased." REFLECTIONS ON JUDGING 43.

The Court has more law clerks, better law clerks, and takes fewer cases — why so much sucking?

> "They have better staff these days too and a lighter workload. Still, why isn't there better output?" *A Conversation with Judge Richard A. Posner*, 58 Duke L. J. 1807, 1811 (2009).

If you want to lose intellectual weight, I recommend a diet of Supreme Court opinions.

> "An exclusive diet of Supreme Court opinions is a recipe for intellectual malnutrition." REFLECTIONS ON JUDGING 83.

I definitely don't want to be on the Supreme Court.

"I just wouldn't enjoy the Supreme Court. Absolutely no desire to be on it." Charney, *How I Write: Richard Posner*.

I wouldn't get to write enough on the Supreme Court.

"Now the Supreme Court justices write very, very few majority opinions. Last year they saw 74 cases. Divide that by 9 and that's a little more than 8 opinions a year. That's ridiculous! I write around 90 opinions a year. I think they get up to an average of about 20 opinions per justice total." Charney, *How I Write: Richard Posner*.

There isn't even enough work for eight Justices.

"I would say rather that the current Court is a very political place, and that the Justices are deficient in career diversity, deficient in understanding science and technology, virtually bereft of trial experience, and underworked." *Michael C. Dorf's "Review" of Richard A. Posner,* Divergent Paths: The Academy and the Judiciary, 166 J. Legal Ed. 203, 207 (2016).

The Supreme Court should assign opinion writing randomly. That's what I do (for the cases I'm not interested in).

> "This problem could be solved by random assignment, among the Justices in the majority in a given case, of responsibility for preparing and circulating the majority opinion." *What is Obviously Wrong II*, 19 Green Bag 2d at 267; "[S]o we split up the case among three judges. Sometimes I assign myself a little more than a third, because I'm selfish." Charney, *How I Write: Richard Posner*.

I have to force myself to read most Supreme Court opinions because they are so tedious.

> "The reason I agreed to write [about Supreme Court cases for Slate] was that it would force me to read more Supreme Court opinions carefully.... They are often tedious, and anyway I find it difficult to get much out of opinions that are not directly relevant to something I'm thinking about. So I thought it would be good for me to read opinions that weren't germane to any case I had—that it would give me a better sense of what's going on in the Supreme Court." Cohen, *An Interview With Judge Richard A. Posner*.

Oh look! A Justice wrote a concurring opinion. *Whoop-de-do!*

"I don't enjoy writing dissenting and concurring opinions, because once the case is decided, there's very little interest in these other opinions." Charney, How I Write: Richard Posner.

The Supreme Court's First Amendment jurisprudence is a joke.

"But to say as judges like to say that in deciding what speech to privilege (adult pornography for example) and what speech to allow to be suppressed they are implementing decisions by the drafters or ratifiers of the Constitution is a joke." What is Obviously Wrong I, 19 Green Bag 2d at 201.

The Supreme Court's decision in *Heller* was pretty bad.

"*Heller v. District of Columbia* and *McDonald v. Chicago* for sure, and going back a few years *Clinton v. Jones* and *Chevron v. Natural Resources Council*." Collins, The Judge & Company (responding to "What do you think is the 'worst' Supreme Court decision of the past decade, and why?").

This Court's best law and economics decision is . . . well, there isn't one.

"A good question, to which I don't have a good answer." Collins, The Judge & Company.

Alito's dissent in *Whole Woman's Health*: Most. Tedious. Ever.

"[T]he most tedious opinion I've ever read. I don't know why I read the whole thing." BookTV, *William Domnarski discusses Richard Posner*, CSPAN (Oct. 4, 2016).

In the past, a lot of shaky Justices slipped in under the radar.

"There has been greater scrutiny. More scrutiny has resulted in candidates with better professional credentials . . . [but] it is not clear that the output is better as a result." *A Conversation with Judge Posner*, 58 Duke L. J. 1807, 1811 (2009).

Cardozo was no saint.

"Cardozo was not a saint." CARDOZO: A STUDY IN REPUTATION 9.

Justice Blackmun spent his time cite checking what his clerks wrote. I can't even.

"Justice Blackmun, a genuine eccentric, after his first few years on the Court left the opinion writing to his law clerks and concentrated on cite checking their drafts." REFLECTIONS ON JUDGING 43.

Justice Douglas was a sourpuss. (Me too I guess.)

"[A]lthough he was a sourpuss, he had a lot of charisma. . . . [H]e was not a 'sweetie.'" Domnarski, 43; "See, I am a sourpuss." BookTV, *William Domnarski discusses Richard Posner*, CSPAN (Oct. 4, 2016).

The Warren Court tried to make bold strides—it fell on its face.

"It's as if the fundamental constitutional law promulgated by the Warren Court were the law of unintended consequences." Domnarski 44.

Despite his too-long neck, Justice Holmes was a great American.

"Not only was Holmes a great jurist, a great prosodist, a great intellectual; he was a great *persona*, a great American, a great life." ESSENTIAL HOLMES xiv-xv.

You have to admit that Holmes had a pretty good line about "three generations of imbeciles."

"[Taking] me to task for praising the rhetoric of Holmes's much criticized opinion in *Buck v. Bell*." THE ESSENTIAL HOLMES xvi-xvii.

The modern trend of crappy dissents is Holmes's fault.

"Unfortunately Holmes' principal legacy as a writer of judicial opinions was not to make well-written opinions fashionable . . . but to make dissent fashionable." THE ESSENTIAL HOLMES xiii-xiv.

Also, Holmes's neck was too long.

"A tall, commanding figure, his looks flawed only (and slightly) by his too-long neck (for which his father liked—nastily—to tease him) . . ." THE ESSENTIAL HOLMES xiv.

I never said the Supreme Court isn't *really a court*. I said it isn't *a real court*. Big difference.

"I thus disagree with Professor Segall's statement that 'our Supreme Court is not really a court at all.'" *What is Obviously Wrong II*, 19 Green Bag 2d at 265 n. 14.

Chapter Seven
AN ECONOMIC ANALYSIS OF CATS

I am rather callous toward the nonfeline population.

> "I think the basic reason I write in a callous tone is that I am rather callous toward the nonfeline population." William Domnarski, RICHARD POSNER 254.

The Hand formula teaches that seeking affection from a cat or an appellate judge will rarely be worth the effort.

> "Indeed, in the example the declaratory judgment will probably foreclose a future suit by the insured against the insurance company, and so the availability of declaratory relief will not have increased the number of cases by even one." ECONOMIC ANALYSIS OF LAW § 22.3 (9th ed. 2014).

My cat Pixie is the only nonsycophant I interact with regularly.

> "Never apologize for strongly stating your case. I am surrounded by sycophants. I don't need that from you." *The Second Life of Judge Richard A. Posner.*

Pixie turned down Harvard College, correctly in my view.

"I would have preferred (mistakenly, as I'm about to note) to go to Harvard." REFLECTIONS ON JUDGING 19.

Ignoring Pixie's advice is usually not worth the risk because the magnitude of harm from cat poop in your slippers is high and also very likely.

"The fact that the burden of precaution is less than the probability times magnitude of loss if the precaution is not taken is a necessary rather than sufficient condition for the precaution to be efficient." ECONOMIC ANALYSIS OF LAW § 6.4 (9th ed. 2014).

Cats are masters of adverse possession.

"For who denies the legitimacy of acquisition of title by adverse possession?" *Samuel C. Johnson 1988 Trust v. Bayfield County*, 649 F.3d 799, 807 (7th Cir. 2011); "Pixie ... lies on my computer keyboard, causing chaos." Jerry Coyne, *Readers' cats: Pixie*, Why Evolution is True.

I do not let law clerks draft my opinions, but I cannot deny Pixie.

> "Pixie is the first one who actually likes me (gives me frequent nuzzles, follows me around, lies on my computer keyboard, causing chaos)." Coyne, *Readers' cats: Pixie*.

Your prior conduct pooping in my slippers is not inadmissible propensity evidence, Pixie. It goes to motive.

> "'Propensity' evidence and 'motive' evidence need not overlap. . . . They do overlap when the crime is motivated by a taste for engaging in that crime or a compulsion to engage in it (an 'addiction'), rather than by a desire for pecuniary gain or for some other advantage to which the crime is instrumental in the sense that it would not be committed if the advantage could be obtained as easily by a lawful route." *United States v. Cunningham*, 103 F.3d 553 (7th Cir. 1996).

Finders keepers is not the law, so I'll have my lap back now, Pixie.

> "The law is not finders keepers, unless the property found has been abandoned, which is to say deliberately relinquished, not merely lost or misplaced." *Employers Ins. of Wausau v. Titan Int'l*, 400 F.3d 486, 491 (7th Cir. 2005).

There are only two million cat videos on the internet. It's not nearly enough.

"In fact, the largest category of websites are cat videos. But still, there are only 2 million cat videos." Zoe Tillman, *Q&A: Judge Posner on Writing, Law School and Cat Videos*, National Law Journal (May 18, 2016).

There is no such thing as *fur curiam*, Pixie.

"She likes to give us nuzzles and be with us." Noah Charney, *How I Write: Richard Posner*, Daily Beast (Nov. 7, 2013).

My cat prefers that I work from home. What can I do?

"Her little face falls if either of us leaves the house. . . . I spend probably at least half the time at home working. . . . One reason is that the cat wants us at home." Charney, *How I Write: Richard Posner*.

Pixie would be a consensus Supreme Court nominee and sail through confirmation.

"What's unusual about her, besides being beautiful and intelligent, but she's affectionate. Very unusual in cats." Charney, *How I Write: Richard Posner*.

Pixie's purr sounds like she's saying *Sanctions*.

"The case for sanctions under Fed. R. App. P. 38 is plain." *Fox Valley AMC/Jeep, Inc. v. AM Credit Corp.*, 836 F.2d 366, 368 (7th Cir. 1988).

A cat's gaze has more wisdom than ten volumes of the U.S. Reports.

"That may seem impertinence on my part, forcing me to invoke the old proverb that 'a cat may look at a king,' one meaning of which is that an inferior is or should be allowed to criticize a superior." *United States v. Dessart*, 823 F.3d 395, 406 (7th Cir. 2016) (concurring opinion).

Pixie is the only family member I will talk about in public. Or to, come to think of it.

"The only member of my family whom I discuss publicly is my cat." Ronald K.L. Collins, *The Man Behind the Robes—A Q&A with Richard Posner*, Concurring Opinions (Dec. 1, 2014).

It's not discrimination that dogs are leashed and licensed but cats roam free. That's the way it should be.

> "Most cities and towns require dogs but not cats to be licensed. There are differences between the animals. Dogs on average are bigger, stronger, and more aggressive than cats, are feared by more people, can give people serious bites, and make a lot of noise outdoors, barking and howling. Feral cats generally are innocuous, and many pet cats are confined indoors." *Illinois Transp. Trade Ass'n v. Chicago*, 839 F.3d 594 (7th Cir. 2016).

Pixie is a harsh editor.

> "But Pixie likes to – when I am typing mostly I have a mouse pad to the right of my eight laptop and I have a wireless mouse. She likes to come over and sit on the wireless mouse. That paralyzed me. If I tried to reach under her she will scratch me. So she enforces precision." BookTV, *William Domnarski discusses Richard Posner*, CSPAN (Oct. 4, 2016).

Pixie doesn't like deferring. Defurring either.

> "What could it mean to say that the district court's decision 'should stand even if we, as an original matter, would have ordered the hearing'?" *United States v. Dessart*, 823 F.3d 395, 406 (7th Cir. 2016) (concurring opinion).

Terrible brief. I lined Pixie's cat box with it and she defecated on the floor.

> "In appellate practice, the lawyers are often quite bad, sometimes awful. I don't understand why." *A Conversation with Judge Richard A. Posner*, 58 Duke L. J. 1807, 1815 (2009).

Chronological age does not coincide with mental or emotional maturity.

What? Why are you looking at me like that, Pixie?

> "Chronological age does not coincide with mental or emotional maturity." REFLECTIONS ON JUDGING 70.

I *am* law and economics.

> "Economic analysis of law has influenced the law in many areas, and also has changed the way law is taught." ECONOMIC ANALYSIS OF LAW xxi (9th ed. 2014).

Pretty sure I've surpassed Hand and Friendly by every empirical measure.

> "[I]t would be fun to test myself against the great judges of the past." Domnarski 25.

Learned Hand never used an exclamation point. Henry Friendly did it once. Me? Three hundred! And counting!!!

> Domnarski 110 ("Over the years he has used the exclamation mark to convey emotions more than three hundred times.").

Judge Friendly wrote about 30 opinions a year. I write *three times* that.

> "Friendly wrote—what?—30 opinions a year; I write three times as many." Domnarski 249.

Learned Hand published less than 2400 appellate opinions. I'm over 3300. *Advantage Poze.*

> "[I]t would be fun to test myself against the great judges of the past." REFLECTIONS ON JUDGING 25.

Henry Friendly had 990 appellate opinions, 808 were majority opinions. Posner has 3300+ appellate opinions, 3000+ majority opinions.

Posner > Friendly *QED.*

> "[I]t would be fun to test myself against the great judges of the past." REFLECTIONS ON JUDGING 25.

AN ECONOMIC ANALYSIS OF CATS

Someone once tried to free ride on my watch by asking what time it was. I said I'd tell him for a nickel. Cheapskate just walked away.

> Domnarski 63 ("A stranger has stopped Dick on the street and asked the time. Dick related that he had said, 'Sure, for a nickel. . . . I explained to him that he could have had his own watch but didn't and was trying to free ride on mine.'").

The most economically efficient use for the *Bluebook* would be to burn every copy for heat during a Chicago winter.

> "A week after all the copies of the *Bluebook* were burned, their absence would not be noticed." REFLECTIONS ON JUDGING 104.

Empirically speaking, it takes two judges to make a hot bench. Also to tango.

> "[E]quilibrium can be destroyed by a seemingly minor change in the environment. So consider a Supreme Court in which all but one or two Justices ask very few questions . . . [and] two very talkative Justices replace two silent ones. The remaining silent Justices may begin to feel uncomfortable." REFLECTIONS ON JUDGING 57.

Economically-minded criminals commit fewer crimes when punishments increase, but I guess criminals aren't that into economics.

> "Although it seems obvious that punishing crime more severely reduces crime rates, even that is uncertain." REFLECTIONS ON JUDGING 60.

Market forces will result in an efficient allocation of drunken strip-joint patrons, with very few being found raising children in residential neighborhoods.

> "[M]uch evidence was presented of the profound incompatibility of a strip joint with the normal activity of the immediate neighborhood, a residential neighborhood whose normal activity is raising kids in a tranquil environment rather than fending off the drunken patrons of a noisy strip joint." *Blue Canary Corp. v. City of Milwaukee*, 251 F.3d 1121, 1125 (7th Cir. 2001).

My empirical research proves that the magnitude of likely harm from slamming other judges isn't greater than the burden of holding back.

> "With these adjustments, the *Dennis* formula becomes $V + E < P \times L/(1 + i)^n$, where n is the number of periods between the utterance of the speech and the resulting harm and i is an interest or discount rate which translates a future dollar of social cost into a present dollar. The larger i and n are, the smaller will be the harm from the speech." *Free Speech in an Economic Perspective*, 20 Suffolk University Law Review 1, 8 (1986).

Still think we should try paying people to have babies for adoption, which is totally different from baby selling.

> "And, by the way, let me take this opportunity to correct the record: neither in the article, nor in my subsequent writing on family law and economics, have I ever advocated 'baby selling.' I have merely pointed out the consequences of the present legal regime, in which monetary transfers incident to adoption are (nominally) capped, and have suggested, by way of experiment only, that some adoption agencies be permitted to pay women contemplating abortion to carry the fetus to term and put the newborn child up for adoption. I continue to think it would be a worthwhile experiment." Bashman, *20 Questions for Circuit Judge Richard A. Posner*.

Economically speaking, fancy belt buckles are a lot like surgical anesthesia.

"The separate market for ornamental buckles resembles the separate market for anesthesia, which exists because a patient can contract separately with the surgeon and with the anesthesiologist." *Jack Walters & Sons Corp. v. Morton Bldg., Inc.*, 737 F.2d 698, 704 (7th Cir. 1984).

Polygamy is unworkable (from an economic perspective).

"Suppose a society contains 100 men and 100 women, but the five wealthiest men have a total of 50 wives. That leaves 95 men to compete for only 50 marriageable women." *Supreme Court Breakfast Table: The chief justice's dissent is heartless*, Slate (June 27, 2015).

In 2008 we learned that American business is really greedy and corrupt. You could've knocked me over with a feather.

[A greater focus on pragmatism over economic analysis] is "partly a result of the economic profession's failure to understand finance and monetary policy in the period leading up to the crash of 2008, and (relatedly) the revelations of unexpected extensive greed and corruption in American business, not limited to the financial industry." Ronald K.L Collins, The Judge & Company – Questions for Judge Posner from Judges, Law Professors & a Journalist, Concurring Opinions (Dec. 3, 2014).

AN ECONOMIC ANALYSIS OF CATS

I was completely wrong about economics. Admitting this shows how right I am about everything else.

> "[I'm] less trustful of purely economic analysis—the last partly because of the crash of 2008 and the ensuing economic downturn. That shook some of my faith in economic analysis." Joel Cohen, *An Interview With Judge Richard A. Posner*, ABA Journal, July 2014.

What price, lost hope (on the open market)?

> "But there is also a big problem of quantifying lost hopes." *Grip-Pak, Inc. v. Illinois Tool Works, Inc.*, 694 F.2d 466, 475 (7th Cir. 1982).

Chapter Eight
NOT IMPRESSED WITH LAW PROFESSORS

I'm not impressed with law professors.

> "But I'm not impressed by law professors' criticisms based on their conception of how judges think, because I don't see how law professors can know how judges think." *What is Obviously Wrong With The Federal Judiciary, Yet Eminently Curable Part II*, 19 Green Bag 2d 257, 262 (2016).

Most law professors are just frustrated grad students from less-lucrative fields.

> "[T]he academy, . . . staffed as it increasingly is with refugees from other disciplines—the graduate students in classics, and history, and anthropology, and so on who upon discovering there were very few well-paying positions in such fields nowadays decided to go to law school and afterward had no time to practice law before getting a law-teaching job." *Supreme Court Breakfast Table: The academy is out of its depth.*

Law professors condescendingly assume federal judges are just dumber versions of them. Actually, federal judges are dumber versions of me.

> "Law professors, not knowing how judges think, mistakenly suppose that judges are weak imitators of law professors, their intellectual superiors." *What is Obviously Wrong II*, 19 Green Bag 2d at 263.

Law schools can improve by hiring people who've had a job besides baby-sitting or running their own lemonade stand.

> "I think law schools should be hiring a higher percentage of lawyers with significant practical experience." *Supreme Court Breakfast Table: The academy is out of its depth.*

Even the best law professors cannot out-stare the average cat.

> "I don't think the Supreme Court is likely to accept advice from law professors on administrative issues, such as whether to have opinions in tie cases and whether to identify the justices voting for or against cert." *Supreme Court Breakfast Table: The academy is out of its depth.*

NOT IMPRESSED WITH LAW PROFESSORS

Law professors think that the Supreme Court cares what they say LOL.

"The court is understandably likely to think that law professors are not in a position to advise on such issues." *Supreme Court Breakfast Table: The academy is out of its depth*, Slate (June 24, 2016).

Like sands through the hourglass, so is the influence of law prof scholarship.

"Many judges think that academics do not understand the aims and pressures of judicial work and that as a result much academic criticism of judicial performance is captious, obtuse, and unconstructive." REFLECTIONS ON JUDGING 205.

Speak all you want, professors, power doesn't listen to the likes of you.

"Amicus briefs? Working for nonprofits? Blogging? 'Speaking truth to power?' Absurd: speak all you want, professors, power doesn't listen to the likes of you." *Supreme Court Breakfast Table: The immigration decision won't do much*, Slate (June 26, 2016).

If the legal academy wants judges to care what they think, they should put on an awards show; the law review articles aren't cutting it.

> "Yet academic critique of judges and judging has little impact these days on judicial behavior." HOW JUDGES THINK 204.

Modern scholarship! Ugh!

> "Modern scholarship! Ugh!" William Domnarski, RICHARD POSNER 247.

The vast bulk of modern legal scholarship not written by me is bullshit.

> "The vast bulk of modern scholarship, in law as in certain other embattled fields of the humanities such as English literature, is *bullshit*." Domnarski 247.

Academic articles about constitutional law and theory are a waste of time.

> "The academics who are wasting their time writing about constitutional law and theory would be more profitably employed either teaching more or conducting research in other areas of law." *The State of Legal Scholarship Today: A Comment on Schlag*, 97 Geo. L. J. 845, 853 (2009).

This paper is interesting: prolix, labored, technically and conceptually flawed. TBH, not actually interesting either.

> "You are, of course, not the first to try to refute the Coase theorem ... I believe your attempt is prolix, labored, and technically and conceptually flawed." Domnarski 64.

Looks like you're trying to write in an impressive style (that means you failed).

> "Well it is nice to have an impressive, arresting style, but when effort to achieve it is perceptible, you've failed." Domnarski 65.

Constitutional theory is generally a bunch of hooey.

> "[C]onstitutional theory (another joke)." *What is Obviously Wrong II*, 19 Green Bag 2d at 265.

I'm sure that law professors do a lot outside the classroom. A lot of nothing.

> "I don't doubt that law professors are frequently active outside the classroom and that their academic work sometimes addresses practical issues, but what I'd like to see is evidence of impact." *Supreme Court Breakfast Table: The immigration decision won't do much.*

The Justices won't listen to law profs asking who voted for certiorari. But they'll listen to me and say how many voted for certiorari.

> "But what could be changed for the better very easily would be . . . the Court's refusal to disclose the vote (not the voters) in cases in which certiorari is denied." *What is Obviously Wrong II*, 19 Green Bag 2d at 266.

The mainstream legal academy doesn't bother to defend its numerous antiquated and pointless practices.

> "The academy rarely bothers to defend any of its antiquated and pointless practices, numerous as they are." *What Is Obviously Wrong With the Federal Judiciary, Yet Eminently Curable Part I*, 19 Green Bag 2d 187, 194 (2016).

The *Bluebook* is a prime example of how *some people* will write innumerable books about ultimately meaningless subjects.

> "There is even a 180-page book called Understanding and Mastering *The Bluebook*. This is beyond parody." REFLECTIONS ON JUDGING 101.

I've hated the *Bluebook* ever since I got reamed out for messing up a cite check in law school.

> "I was called on the carpet by Peter Edelman, the Review's managing editor, for having performed a deficient 'technical citecheck' on an article or note. He was quite savage in his criticisms, and I worried, though it turned out unnecessarily, that his criticisms would result in my being passed over for the presidency [of the Harvard Law Review]." *The Bluebook Blues*, 120 Yale L. J. 850, 856 n. 9 (2011).

Harvard Law Review editors are literally and figuratively drunk on revenues from the *Bluebook*.

> "The growth in the *Bluebook*'s length is probably attributable in part to the desire, largely financial in origin, to issue editions at short intervals." REFLECTIONS ON JUDGING 103 & n. 103.

Nobody even tries to answer my criticism of the *Bluebook*. As if I'm the one who's going on pointlessly ad nauseum about trivialities.

> "The *Bluebook* must have its defenders—let them defend their precious tome from me." *What is Obviously Wrong II*, 19 Green Bag 2d at 268.

You'll find my criticism of the *Bluebook* on Wikipedia, but not any responses. Typical of the mainstream legal academy.

> "If you look up 'Bluebook' in Wikipedia, you find under 'reception' a summary of my criticisms; but you find no defenses. That however is typical of legal academia." *What Is Obviously Wrong I*, 19 Green Bag 2d at 194.

Rejecting the *Bluebook* is not enough. It must be burned.

> "[T]he first thing to do is burn all copies of the *Bluebook*." *What Is Obviously Wrong I*, 19 Green Bag 2d at 193.

Chapter Nine
THIS ARGUMENT, IT'S FEEBLE[*]

Bad lawyers are bad for justice. Talented lawyers are even worse.

"There are simply too many people spending their time on these zero-marginal-social-product activities. Worse, many of them are highly talented." *What Is Obviously Wrong With the Federal Judiciary, Yet Eminently Curable Part I*, 19 Green Bag 2d 187, 191 (2016).

Lawyers are overly formal and nitpicky. Because of the *Bluebook*.

"[C]ite checking (for conformity to citation format, as distinct from ensuring substantive accuracy) distracts law students and lawyers from legal analysis and breeds a culture of formalism, nitpicking, and manual gazing." REFLECTIONS ON JUDGING 58.

---

[*] *Wolf v. Walker* (Oral argument Aug. 26, 2014).

Don't use collateral estoppel to punish a lawyer. There are better ways.

"Collateral estoppel is not properly invoked to punish a lawyer." *Grip-Pak, Inc. v. Ill. Tool Works, Inc.*, 694 F.2d 466, 469 (7th Cir. 1982).

An important writing lesson: If you don't have style, don't even try.

"People not gifted with a sense of style, you and me for example, should strive to write unaffectedly and plainly." William Domnarski, RICHARD POSNER 65.

Do not include irrelevant facts like dates in a brief's fact section. Do include irrelevant facts the appellate judge might wonder about.

"[D]ates, for example, where nothing turns on the date of a particular occurrence." Foreword, Robert F. Blomquist, THE QUOTABLE JUDGE POSNER, SELECTIONS FROM TWENTY-FIVE YEARS OF JUDICIAL OPINIONS (1996).

You say expert, I say crank.

"Martens' was the testimony either of a crank or, what is more likely, of a man who is making a career out of testifying for plaintiffs in automobile accident cases in which a door may have opened; at the time of trial he was involved in 10 such cases." *Chaulk v. Volkswagen of America, Inc.*, 808 F.2d 639, 644 (7th Cir. 1986).

Prisoners better disclose the full extent of their ramen stash or I'll deny *in forma pauperis* status.

"The account had a balance of about $1400 when the plaintiff applied for leave to proceed *in forma pauperis*—not the 'approximately $10' that he had claimed was all the money he had in 'all checking, savings, prison, or other accounts.'" *Kennedy v. Huibregtse*, 831 F.3d 441, 443 (7th Cir. 2016).

Soothing noises usually are not a basis for equitable estoppel.

"If the victim of a breach of fiduciary duty can and should sue when he discovers the breach rather than later, when he is injured by the breach, then soothing noises probably are not a basis for equitable estoppel in these cases because the noises do not interfere with the fraud victim's ability to sue. So once again the plaintiffs' argument for a longer period in which to sue fails." *Wolin v. Smith Barney Inc.*, 83 F.3d 847, 855 (7th Cir. 1996).

No rent, no expenses: a prisoner with $2000 is riding on Easy Street.

"But this is misleading because the prison provides prisoners with food, clothing, shelter, medical care, and protection (albeit often spotty) against criminal assault, making the plaintiff's entire $2000+ available to finance his lawsuit." *Kennedy v. Huibregtse*, 831 F.3d 441, 443 (7th Cir. 2016).

How long do we have to put up with prisoner lawsuits?

"However, unless and until either Congress or the Supreme Court changes the ground rules that have evolved for this type of litigation, all judicial officers in this circuit must exert themselves to handle prisoner cases in conscientious compliance with these rules, complex as the rules have become." *Del Raine v. Carlson*, 826 F.2d 698, 702 (7th Cir. 1987)

Prisoners should be thinking about what they did to get in prison, not dreaming up new frivolous lawsuits about their imprisonment.

"However dubious—bizarre, even—it might seem as an original matter to allow lawfully imprisoned convicts to spend their time bringing damage suits against their jailers, so that instead of reflecting on the wrongs they have done to society our convicts—exchanging as it were contrition for indignation—prosecute an endless series of mostly imaginary grievances against society, this branch of federal jurisdiction is too well established for me to question it and I do not, but merely record in passing my amazement that it has been allowed to grow to its present extent." *McKeever v. Israel*, 689 F.2d 1315, 1323 (7th Cir. 1982).

Class action lawyers are no more than professional racketeers.

"The type of class action illustrated by this case—the class action that yields fees for class counsel and nothing for the class—is no better than a racket. It must end." *In re Walgreen Co. Stockholder Litig.*, 832 F.3d 718, 724 (7th Cir. 2016).

Moral turpitude has no meaning. None.

"The Board should not be blamed too harshly; courts have equally failed to impart a clear meaning to 'moral turpitude.' Time has only confirmed Justice Jackson's powerful dissent in the *De George* case, in which he called 'moral turpitude' an 'undefined and undefinable standard.' 341 U.S. at 235. The term may well have outlived its usefulness." *Mei v. Ashcroft*, 393 F.3d 737, 741 (7th Cir. 2004).

Don't rely on party experts. They rarely know how to really party.

"I am a big fan of Federal Rule of Evidence 706, which allows a judge to appoint his own expert witness, as opposed to having to depend entirely on party experts." Ronald K.L Collins, *The Judge & Company–Questions for Judge Posner from Judges, Law Professors & a Journalist*, Concurring Opinions (Dec. 3, 2014).

The Fourth Amendment doesn't require or even prefer warrants, dummies.

"[T]he Fourth Amendment doesn't say or suggest that warrants to search or arrest are *ever* required." *What is Obviously Wrong With The Federal Judiciary, Yet Eminently Curable Part II*, 19 Green Bag 2d 257, 258 (2016).

$21,000 is an irrational amount to award for emotional distress.

$10,500 is more like it.

"An award of $ 21,000 is too much for a moment's pang of distress at being fired. . . . [A] remittitur of $10,500 in damages for emotional distress (half the award) is necessary to keep the award of these damages within the limits of the rational." *Avitia v. Metropolitan Club*, 49 F.3d 1219, 1229–1230 (7th Cir. 1995).

Chapter Ten
THE ADVERSARY SYSTEM IS OVERRATED[*]

John Roberts shouldn't be so smug about our legal system, at least not about the non-Posner parts.

"Chief Justice Roberts in his annual reports likes to describe the American legal system as the envy of the world. Nonsense." *What Is Obviously Wrong With the Federal Judiciary, Yet Eminently Curable Part I*, 19 Green Bag 2d 187, 188 (2016).

---

[*] "I think the adversary system is overrated." Ronald K.L. Collins, *The Judge & Company–Questions for Judge Posner from Judges, Law Professors & a Journalist,* Concurring Opinions (Dec. 3, 2014).

The Magna Carta, really?

"You don't hear doctors bragging about thirteenth-century medicine, but you hear lawyers bragging about the thirteenth-century Magna Carta." *What Is Obviously Wrong I*, 19 Green Bag 2d at 188.

The inquisitorial system would be better than our adversarial system (with the right judge).

"Not that I want to convert to the inquisitorial system that prevails in Europe (except the U.K.) and most of the rest of the world, but I want to see the adversary system taken down a peg." Collins, *The Judge & Company*.

Studying the Constitution – what's the point of *that*?

"I see absolutely no value to a judge of spending decades, years, months, weeks, day, hours, minutes, or seconds studying the Constitution, the history of its enactment, its amendments, and its implementation." *Supreme Court Breakfast Table: The academy is out of its depth*, Slate (June 24, 2016).

Legal doctrine is overrated.

"I think the role of legal doctrine in judicial decisions is considerably overrated." Collins, *The Judge & Company*.

Originalism is nonsense.

"And so 'originalism' is nonsense." *What is Obviously Wrong With The Federal Judiciary, Yet Eminently Curable Part II*, 19 Green Bag 2d 257, 258 (2016).

Originalism has no answer to the Maine Coon.

"I have a Maine Coon cat - half raccoon. Her name is Dinah. She was in the New Yorker." *The Second Life of Judge Richard A. Posner*.

If textualism is so neutral, must be a coincidence that it supports Scalia's conservative political preferences so often.

"Another curious feature of Scalia's defense of his judicial votes as being untainted by political ideology is that most of the liberal judicial votes that he mentions are dissents from conservative decisions and so have no impact on the conservative result." REFLECTIONS ON JUDGING 184–185.

It is impossible to know the meaning of anything using a dictionary. Even the definition of circular is circular.

"Dictionaries are mazes in which judges are soon lost." REFLECTIONS ON JUDGING 200.

A dictionary-centered textualism is hopeless.

"A dictionary-centered textualism is hopeless." *The Incoherence of Antonin Scalia*, New Republic (Aug. 24, 2012).

A taco bowl is a sandwich.

"[A] hamburger is regarded as a sandwich, and also a hot dog—and some people regard tacos and burritos as sandwiches, and a quesadilla is even more sandwich-like." *The Incoherence of Antonin Scalia*.

The common law wafts in and out of Scalia and Garner's textualism like flatulence after a bad taco sandwich.

"Notice how the common law wafts unpredictably in and out of their analysis." REFLECTIONS ON JUDGING 213.

Bryan Garner tried to clarify "proximate cause" in the latest Black's Law Dictionary. He failed.

"The effort at clarification is a flop." REFLECTIONS ON JUDGING 66.

Canons of construction are for pompous windbags.

"[A] pompous term for principles of interpretation." REFLECTIONS ON JUDGING 58.

The canons of construction are as outdated as real cannons and far more dangerous.

"[T]he canons of statutory construction (which are a joke)." *What is Obviously Wrong II*, 19 Green Bag 2d at 265.

Pattern jury instructions assume juries are far stupider than they really are.

"The problem is that, being drafted in legal language, many pattern instructions are largely unintelligible to jurors. The drafters appear to have a deficient sense of the capabilities of the intended audience." *What Is Obviously Wrong I*, 19 Green Bag 2d at 189.

I tell juries not to do their own internet research. With a straight face.

"I also make sure to give the jurors reasons for what I tell them not to do, such as not to do their own Internet research." *What Is Obviously Wrong I*, 19 Green Bag 2d at 189.

If juries do internet research: chaos. If appellate judges do it: no biggie. I fail to see a conflict.

> "Trials would become downright chaotic." "I said that jurors shouldn't be permitted to do Internet research, but the judge should be." *What Is Obviously Wrong I*, 19 Green Bag 2d at 189, 193.

With Wikipedia, who needs experts?

> "When medical information can be gleaned from the websites of highly reputable medical centers, it is not imperative that it instead be presented by a testifying witness." *Rowe v. Gibson*, 798 F.3d 622, 628 (7th Cir. 2015).

Stodginess and stuffiness are our biggest problems in the judiciary.

> "The most serious problem with appellate litigation, both at the circuit level and in the Supreme Court . . . is the stodginess and stuffiness of the American legal culture." *What is Obviously Wrong I*, 19 Green Bag 2d at 199.

Unlike most of the federal judiciary I don't fetishize adversary procedure. I fetishize cats.

"This is not the case in which to fetishize adversary procedure. . . . It is heartless to make a fetish of adversary procedure if by doing so feeble evidence is credited because the opponent has no practical access to offsetting evidence." *Rowe v. Gibson*, 798 F.3d 622, 629, 630 (7th Cir. 2015).

You can't take the hearsay rule seriously.

"As with much of the folk psychology of evidence, it is difficult to take this rationale entirely seriously, since people are entirely capable of spontaneous lies in emotional circumstances." *Lust v. Sealy*, 383 F.3d 580, 588 (7th Cir. 2004).

Appellate standards of review are a sham. I don't know why we bother asking for them.

"If my analysis is correct, there is no reason for an appellate opinion to mention a standard of review." *What Is Obviously Wrong I*, 19 Green Bag 2d at 198.

The pragmatist judge can safely ignore precedent.

"[J]udges not constrained by the threat of reversal of their decisions by a higher court would tend to depart more frequently from deciding according to precedent than courts that were so constrained, and that this would show up in a lower depreciation rate of their citations (because they would be giving less weight to the recency of the precedents cited)." *Legal Precedent: A Theoretical and Empirical Analysis*, 19 J. Law & Econ. 249 (1976) (with William A. Landes).

What has precedent done for you lately?

"Yet whether a precedent is recent or ancient, it is entitled to weight apart from its intrinsic merit only if ignoring or rejecting it would upset reasonable expectations without generating equivalent or greater benefits." *What is Obviously Wrong II*, 19 Green Bag 2d at 260.

Patent law is a failure.

"The result is a significant legal and regulatory failure." REFLECTIONS ON JUDGING 75.

The Federal Circuit is effectively a court of immigration judges.

"At the federal level, the specialized court or court-like administrative agency has been a flop." REFLECTIONS ON JUDGING 94.

Constructive possession — what a crock.

> "What can 'constructive' possession of the contents of one's own apartment mean?" REFLECTIONS ON JUDGING 261.

A judge with empathy is doing it wrong.

> "Judges do not have the time or the emotional resilience to become empathetically involved with the parties to litigation." William Domnarski, RICHARD POSNER 142.

If you don't lose your humanity after being a judge for a while, you probably weren't human to start with.

> "Just as doctors tend to be callous about sick people, judges tend to be callous about pathetic litigants because they have seen so many of them." HOW JUDGES THINK 119.

The pragmatist judge expressly discounts the possibility of Elvish involvement when deciding a case.

"Elves may have played ninepins with the jar of peanuts while Welge and Godfrey were sleeping; but elves could remove a jar of peanuts from a locked cupboard. The plaintiff in a products liability suit is not required to exclude every possibility, however fantastic or remote, that the defect which led to the accident was caused by someone other than one of the defendants." *Welge v. Planters Lifesavers Co.*, 17 F.3d 209, 210 (1994).

Clear error, substantial evidence, abuse of discretion: most judges are too stupid to distinguish them.

"But the last three are, in practice, the same, because finer distinctions are beyond judges' cognitive capacity." REFLECTIONS ON JUDGING 251.

If judges don't understand statistics, how will they understand lies and damn lies?

"Notice the non sequitur: because judges don't understand statistics, statistics can't prove a systematic behavioral difference between men and women." REFLECTIONS ON JUDGING 81.

Judges should be taught how ridiculous the legislative process is so they will be more comfortable legislating from the bench.

> "[M]ost legislators have a very limited time horizon-the next election. This reduces their incentive to invest time and effort in crafting far-sighted legislation. Clearly then, the legislators need 'agents in application,' who are, of course, the judges." *Legislation and Its Interpretation: A Primer*, 68 Nebraska Law Review 431, 439 (1989).

Legal writing should be simple but it's not. I denominate this problem to be one of terminological complexity.

> "I think there is no need for terminological complexity in law. I think everything we do, the judges do, can be expressed in ordinary English." Zoe Tillman, *Q&A: Judge Posner on Writing, Law School and Cat Videos*, National Law Journal (May 18, 2016).

The Fourth Amendment never ever ever requires warrants. Like, ever.

> "Nothing in the amendment requires warrants—ever." *United States v. Dessart*, 823 F.3d 395 (2016) (concurring opinion); "I like contemporary popular music a lot — Kelly Clarkson, Sara Bareilles, Taylor Swift, Adele, OneRepublic, Bruno Mars, etc." Ronald K.L. Collins, The Man Behind the Robes—A Q&A with Richard Posner (Dec. 1, 2014).

Trial lawyers should develop the record by speculating about what idiosyncratic appellate judges might be curious about.

> "Brother Jim's case illustrates lawyers' failure to anticipate and answer questions that are likely to occur to appellate judges." REFLECTIONS ON JUDGING 139.

What's so great about deference?

> "First is the proposition that when a judge issues a warrant, whether to search or to arrest, the appellate court must afford 'great deference' to the issuing judge's conclusion that there was probable cause. ... Why *great* deference?" *United States v. Dessart*, 823 F.3d 395 (2016) (concurring opinion).

More abuse of discretion? Hasn't discretion suffered enough?

"And 'abuse' seems altogether too strong a term to describe what may be no more than a disagreement between equally competent judges—the trial judge and the appellate judges—that the appellate judges happen to be empowered to resolve as they see fit." *United States v. Dessart*, 823 F.3d 395 (7th Cir. 2016) (concurring opinion).

Chapter Eleven
I BLAME THE LAW CLERKS

One of the most intractable problems with the federal judiciary, if not the most, is law clerks.

> "But what could be changed for the better very easily would be . . . the excessive reliance on law clerks." *What is Obviously Wrong With The Federal Judiciary, Yet Eminently Curable Part II*, 19 Green Bag 2d 257, 266 (2016).

If it weren't for law clerks we would have much better judges.

> "And the Supreme Court Justices, and many of the court of appeals judges, have really good law clerks; they're really smart. So the politicians figure, 'well, we're appointing this person; doesn't have much experience—never been in a trial courtroom, for example—but there are all these brilliant law clerks working, so their opinions will be all right, because the law clerks will write them.'" BookTV, *William Domnarski discusses Richard Posner*, CSPAN (Oct. 4, 2016).

OTOH, career law clerks are a good idea for weak judges who can't handle the job on their own.

> "Except for very weak judges, having a career clerk is a mistake, as it tempts the judge to delegate excessively to that clerk because of his or her experience." REFLECTIONS ON JUDGING 34.

As law clerks get better and better, Supreme Court nominees get worse and worse.

> "The abler a judge's staff, the less emphasis the appointing authorities need place on the judge's ability, because . . . he can hide behind the staff, delegating opinion writing to staff and relying heavily on staff for advice on how to vote." REFLECTIONS ON JUDGING 53.

Making exploding offers to law-clerk applicants is very wrong. Especially when they have an interview lined up with me.

> "I think it *very* wrong for judges to make exploding offers (that is setting a deadline, often no more than an hour or two and sometimes much less, for the applicant's response to the judge's offer of a clerkship)." REFLECTIONS ON JUDGING 34.

I BLAME THE LAW CLERKS

I don't hire law clerks because I like them. If I did it would be harder to treat them like this.

> "To select law clerks on personal grounds, such as ... the fact that the applicant is ... charming, personable, or good looking, is therefore inappropriate." REFLECTIONS ON JUDGING 34.

Note to self: Law clerks are not personal servants.

> "I think it is important to impress on judges that law clerks are not personal servants." REFLECTIONS ON JUDGING 33.

I have a carefully detailed regimen for training law clerks. It begins with introducing them to the "clerk hook."

> "I want them to be *entirely* candid and direct with me (brutally so if they want)." REFLECTIONS ON JUDGING 128.

Cruel and unusual is relative, I tell my law clerks.

> "The term 'cruel and unusual punishments' is relative rather than absolute." *Davenport v. Derobertis*, 844 F.2d 1310, 1315 (7th Cir. 1988).

Posner Thoughts, *Annotated*

I don't cry and neither do my law clerks if they know what's good for them.

"I don't cry! I don't like grim books or movies, so I steer clear of them. I don't like emotional things. Adventure is fine, but I don't like things that are sad." Noah Charney, *How I Write: Richard Posner*, Daily Beast (Nov. 7, 2013).

My law clerks are not allowed to pussyfoot. That privilege is reserved for Pixie.

"If they think I'm wrong about something, I want them to tell me I'm wrong, with no pussy-footing." REFLECTIONS ON JUDGING 128.

Sleep is for people who are not my law clerks.

"I don't take vacations. ... So I work weekends, nights. I have lots of time and I write. I am fast, I cover a lot of ground." Charney, *How I Write: Richard Posner*.

Other judges' decisions are poorly written. I blame the law clerks.

"I think opinions have become longer, more formalistic, and more uniform, also less colorful and less individual, as a result of the near-universal delegation of opinion writing to law clerks." Ronald K.L Collins, *The Judge & Company – Questions for Judge Posner from Judges, Law Professors & a Journalist*, Concurring Opinions (Dec. 3, 2014).

The law clerks who wrote Scalia's book should be embarrassed.

> "His book has errors. I connect that in part to the fact that in the front of the book there are acknowledgments of assistance from more than 90 people, including a number of law students. My guess is that much of the book was written by research assistants and was not adequately checked." Joel Cohen, *An Interview With Judge Richard A. Posner*, ABA Journal (July 2014).

Letting law clerks write opinions is seductive like the Dark Side. Weak judges give in.

> "I can see, however, how a weak judge would find the model irresistible." REFLECTIONS ON JUDGING 129.

Law clerks are slow.

> "A judge who writes his own opinions will achieve speed, whereas law clerks, as inexperienced opinion writers fearful of making a bad impression on the judge, will waste a lot of time as opinion writers." Collins, *The Judge & Company*.

Law clerks' writing. Save me.

> "Clerk-written opinions tend to a dreary uniformity and often fail to disclose the considerations that actually moved the court to its decision." Bashman, *20 Questions for Circuit Judge Richard A. Posner*.

Judicial opinions should have more of the judge, less of the sludge.

"To read a judicial opinion written by a law clerk is often like navigating a muddy, tumid stream. A typical such opinion might start with a detailed recitation of the facts, many of them irrelevant as well as uninteresting (dates, for example, where nothing turns on the date of a particular occurrence)." Foreword, Robert F. Blomquist, THE QUOTABLE JUDGE POSNER, SELECTIONS FROM TWENTY-FIVE YEARS OF JUDICIAL OPINIONS (1996).

More law clerks means less justice.

"An unnecessary increase in staff not only is a waste of money but also may cause a fall in quality, not of the clerks but of the judge's output." REFLECTIONS ON JUDGING 52.

I BLAME THE LAW CLERKS

Law clerks and fashion models are equally useful.

Mitchell v. JCG Indus., Inc., 753 F.3d 695 (7th Cir. 2014) (image below).

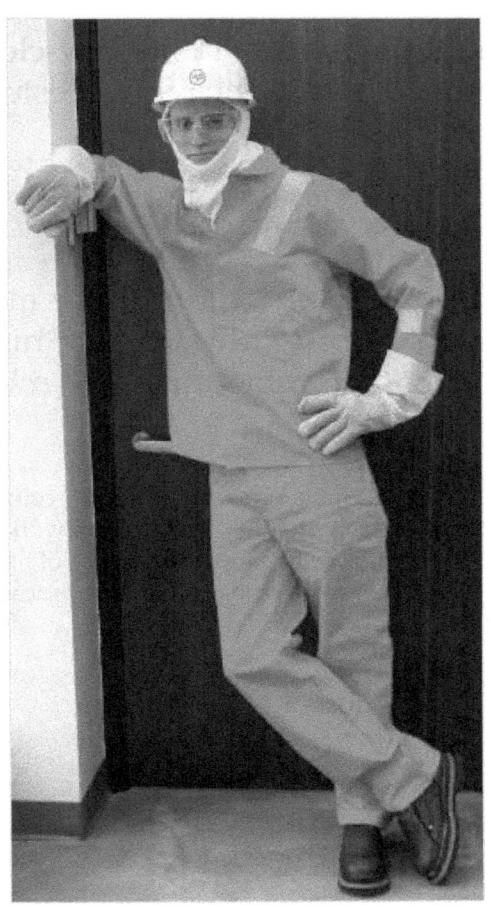

I hold the models in my law-clerk fashion shows in the highest esteem.

> "Because I don't think law clerks should write judicial opinions, it may seem that I hold them in low esteem. Not at all." REFLECTIONS ON JUDGING 127–128.

Thank God Holmes didn't have modern law clerks to prop him up past his time like the iconic protagonist of *Weekend at Bernie's*.

> "[A]lthough his mind remained sharp, he could no longer handle his share of the Court's workload and, God be praised, the modern practice of having law clerks ghostwrite opinions had not yet caught on." ESSENTIAL HOLMES xi.

Chapter Twelve
WHAT HORRIBLE STUFF*

The unedited thoughts that run through people's minds are pretty strange.

> "[T]he unedited thoughts that run through people's mind[s] are pretty strange." *United States v. Tucker*, 773 F.2d 136, 140 (7th Cir. 1985).

You can patent margarine. Who knew?

> "There is nutritional biochemistry, which, I have learned from a recent case that I handled involving a patent on a margarine product, can be even more complex than some areas of computer science." REFLECTIONS ON JUDGING 72.

---

* *Wolf v. Walker* (Oral argument Aug. 26, 2014).

It's too expensive to keep old sex offenders in jail. How many more offenses could they have in them?

"Last year, only 1,451 men ages sixty-five and older were arrested for sex offenses, which was fewer than 3 percent of the total number of arrests of male sex offenders that year." REFLECTIONS ON JUDGING 69–70.

Margarine is harder to understand than computer science.

"There is nutritional biochemistry, which, I have learned from a recent case that I handled involving a patent on a margarine product, can be even more complex than some areas of computer science." REFLECTIONS ON JUDGING 72.

Eiusdem, not *ejustem*!

"[E]*iusdem generis* (which lawyers misspell as *ejusdem generis* because that's how English judges spelled it ages ago)." REFLECTIONS ON JUDGING 205.

No amicus curiae has ever sent me a birthday card.

"[I]t is very rare for an amicus curiae brief to do more than repeat in somewhat different language the arguments in the brief of the party whom the amicus is supporting. Those who pay lawyers to prepare such briefs are not getting their money's worth." *Voices for Choices v. Illinois Bell Telephone Co.*, 339 F.3d 542, 545 (7th Cir. 2003).

Privacy is another way to say lying about yourself.

"Privacy is wanted by people because they want to conceal information to fool others." *Privacy is Overrated*, NY Daily News (April 28, 2014).

Google is your friend, and a much better one than any so-called amicus.

"[A]micus briefs, often solicited by parties, may be used to make an end run around court-imposed limitations on the length of parties' briefs; the time and other resources required for the preparation and study of, and response to, amicus briefs drive up the cost of litigation; and the filing of an amicus brief is often an attempt to inject interest group politics into the federal appeals process." *Voices for Choices v. Illinois Bell Telephone Co.*, 339 F.3d 542, 544 (7th Cir. 2003).

The difference between ordinary criminals and those with addled brains is that we don't hate the addled ones.

"We punish criminals because we fear and (most of us) hate them, not because of what we can find inside their heads. If the defendant's brain is so addled that we think him a victim along with his victim, we no longer hate him but we still fear him." REFLECTIONS ON JUDGING 74.

Who even knew there were Jehovah's Witnesses in Eritrea?

"Who even knew there were Jehovah's Witnesses in Eritrea?" REFLECTIONS ON JUDGING 82.

Multifactor tests are a crutch for bewildered judges.

"Second, appellate courts adopt multifactor tests for the trial court to apply." REFLECTIONS ON JUDGING 85–86.

Wear shoes when seeking judicial review.

"The path to judicial review is strewn with thorns." *Attorney Registration & Disciplinary Commission of Supreme Court v. Schweiker*, 715 F.2d 282, 286 (7th Cir. 1983).

WHAT HORRIBLE STUFF

I'm not in favor of deference, but with all the murderers and rapists and whatnot, when it comes how you run a prison, defer away.

> "Recently we noted that Pontiac is a den of murderers, rapists, and others with no respect for the law—and all too often nothing to lose from further mayhem. We have therefore insisted that district judges in this circuit give great though not complete deference to the decisions of the prison authorities on matters affecting the maintenance of order." *Azeez v. Fairman*, 795 F.2d 1296, 1298 (7th Cir. 1986).

You can be rambling and weird but still not demented.

> "The letter in question is rambling, weird, but not demented." *United States v. Tucker*, 773 F.2d 136, 140 (7th Cir. 1985).

You can't get habeas corpus if the defendant doesn't habeas your corpus.

> "The habeas corpus statute does not say who shall be named as respondent in a habeas corpus petition but implies, quite naturally since habeas corpus challenges the lawfulness of the petitioner's custody, that it shall be the person who has that custody." *Reimnitz v. State's Attorney of Cook Cty.*, 761 F.2d 405, 408 (7th Cir. 1985).

Hey there reader! You still paying attention?

"The alert reader will wonder, though, whether we can end the analysis here. Shouldn't we consider loss as well as knowledge?" *Wolin v. Smith Barney Inc.*, 83 F.3d 847, 853 (7th Cir. 1996).

Big judges don't cry.

"An award of $ 21,000 is too much for a moment's pang of distress at being fired, even distress enough to make a grown man cry who believes—and we do not mean to criticize such a belief—that crying is shameful in a man." *Avitia v. Metropolitan Club*, 49 F.3d 1219, 1229 (7th Cir. 1995).

Multifactor tests are how appellate judges shirk.

"The sensible thing would be to apply that standard directly rather than apply a multifactor test. But that would leave less discretion to the trial court and thus make more work for the appellate judges." REFLECTIONS ON JUDGING 87.

Are judges sheep? Ironically, this keeps me up at night.

"Are judges sheep? Why should they care what kids at the Harvard Law Review consider proper abbreviation?" REFLECTIONS ON JUDGING 99.

Privacy is for your pants. Everything else is fair game.

"'Privacy' is really just a euphemism for concealment, for hiding specific things about ourselves from others." *Privacy is overrated*, NY Daily News (April 28, 2013).

You can point both cannons and canons in any direction you wish.

"[T]he two canons [i.e., the "last-antecedent" canon and the "series-qualifier" canon] contradict each other." REFLECTIONS ON JUDGING 208.

Live by technicalities, die by technicalities.

"The bringers of suit based on technicalities will not be heard to complain about defenses based on technicalities." *Wolin v. Smith Barney Inc.*, 83 F.3d 847, 856 (7th Cir. 1996).

Blowing up an electric pylon isn't terrorism. Blowing up an electoral pile-on is another thing.

"I would prefer to confine the term to situations in which the actual or intended harm is very great. I would therefore exclude ecoterrorism and animal rights terrorism. . . . So far, though, my impression is that ecoterrorists just like to blow up electrical pylons." *The Second Life of Judge Richard A. Posner*.

Swing state voters deserve to choose the president.

"They are likely to be the most thoughtful voters, on average (and for the further reason that they will have received the most information and attention from the candidates), and the most thoughtful voters should be the ones to decide the election." *In Defense of the Electoral College*, Slate (Nov. 12, 2012).

"Goofy" describes a cartoon dog, the Republican Party, and the Supreme Court from 1967 to 1981.

"I was surprised to learn how many goofy constitutional decisions had been rendered in the intervening fourteen years." REFLECTIONS ON JUDGING 33; "I've become less conservative since the Republican Party started becoming goofy." Nina Totenberg, *Federal Judge Richard Posner: The GOP Has Made Me Less Conservative*, NPR (July 5, 2012).

Yale Law School is for babies.

"[I] decided that Harvard would be the greater challenge; it didn't baby the students, as Yale Law School did and does." REFLECTIONS ON JUDGING 20.

If I weren't a judge I could tell you what I *really* think.

"I would be more outspoken about what seem to be serious failings of American government, including the judiciary." Collins, *The Judge & Company*.

Enough!

"Enough!" *Nicolet Instrument Corp. v. Lindquist & Vennum*, 34 F.3d 453, 456 (7th Cir. 1994).

Appendix:
THINGS THAT ARE OVERRATED
(A partial list)

1. Privacy.

    Privacy is overrated, NY Daily News (April 28, 2013).

2. The adversary system.

    "I think the adversary system is overrated." Ronald K.L. Collins, The Judge & Company – Questions for Judge Posner from Judges, Law Professors & a Journalist, Concurring Opinions (Dec. 3, 2014).

3. Legal doctrine.

    "I think the role of legal doctrine in judicial decisions is considerably overrated." Collins, The Judge & Company.

4. The Magna Carta.

    "You don't hear doctors bragging about thirteenth-century medicine, but you hear lawyers bragging about the thirteenth-century Magna Carta." *What Is Obviously Wrong I*, 19 Green Bag 2d at 188.

5. Judicial deliberation.

    "And judicial deliberation is overrated as a means of bringing about agreement on issues that divide judges deeply, as constitutional issues often do." REFLECTIONS ON JUDGING 171.

6. Legalism.

    HOW JUDGES THINK 7–9, 41–56.

7. Justice Cardozo and Chief Justice John Marshall (as stylists, somewhat).

    "Regarding Weisberg and White's analyses of opinions by Cardozo and Marshall, limitations of space and time prevent my doing more than registering the view that, as stylists, these great judges have been somewhat overrated." *Law and Literature: A Relation Reargued*, 72 Va. L. Rev. 1351, 1385–1386 (1986).

8. *A Man For All Seasons* (the movie).

    "On the debit side of the law-film ledger one finds that overrated costume drama *A Man for All Seasons* (1966)." LAW AND LITERATURE 53.

BIBLIOGRAPHY

By Richard A. Posner: books

Aging and Old Age (1995)
An Affair of State (1999)
The Behavior of Federal Judges: A Theoretical and Empirical Study of Rational Choice (with Lee Epstein & William M. Landes) (2013)
Cardozo: A Study in Reputation (1990)
Economic Analysis of Law (9th ed. 2014)
The Essential Holmes (1992)
The Federal Judiciary: Strengths and Weaknesses (2017)
How Judges Think (2008)
Law and Literature (1988)
Law, Pragmatism, and Democracy (2003)
Overcoming Law (1995)
Reflections on Judging (2013)

Articles

Against Footnotes, 38 J. American Judges Ass'n 24 (2001)
The Bluebook *Blues,* 120 Yale L. J. 850 (2011)
The Decline and Fall of AT&T: A Personal Recollection, 61 FCC L. J. 11 (2008)
The Depiction of Law in The Bonfire of the Vanities, 98 Yale L. J. 1653 (1989)
Effective Appellate Brief Writing, Litigation News (Spring 2010)
Free Speech in an Economic Perspective, 20 Suffolk Univ. L. Rev. 1 (1986)
Homosexual Marriage, Becker-Posner Blog (May 13, 2012), bit.ly/2g9hdEg
In Defense of the Electoral College, Slate (Nov. 12, 2012), slate.me/2fziWCA
The Incoherence of Antonin Scalia, New Republic (Aug. 24, 2012)
Judicial Biography, 70 N.Y.U. L. Rev. 502 (2013)

Posner Thoughts, *Annotated*

Law and Literature: A Relation Reargued,
   72 Va. L. Rev. 1351 (1986)
Legal Precedent: A Theoretical and Empirical Analysis,
   19 J. Law & Econ. 249 (1976) (with William A. Landes)
Legislation and Its Interpretation: A Primer,
   68 Nebraska L. Rev. 431 (1989)
Michael C. Dorf's "Review" of Richard A. Posner, Divergent Paths:
   The Academy and the Judiciary, 166 J. Legal Ed. 203 (2016)
Privacy is overrated, NY Daily News (April 28, 2013),
   bit.ly/Posner-privacy
The State of Legal Scholarship Today: A Comment on Schlag,
   97 Geo. L. J. 845 (2009)
The Supreme Court and Celebrity Culture,
   88 Chicago-Kent L. Rev. 299 (2013)
Supreme Court Breakfast Table: The academy is out of its depth,
   Slate (June 24, 2016), slate.me/2fTBjFf
Supreme Court Breakfast Table: The chief justice's dissent is heartless, Slate (June 27, 2015), slate.me/2ftLtfa
Supreme Court Breakfast Table: The immigration decision won't do much, Slate (June 26, 2016), slate.me/2gVCOUz
Supreme Court Year in Review: Chief Justice Roberts did the right thing—but it's still a bad law, Slate (June 29, 2012),
   slate.me/2gluYmd
What Is Obviously Wrong With the Federal Judiciary, Yet Eminently Curable Part I, 19 Green Bag 2d 187 (2016)
What is Obviously Wrong With The Federal Judiciary, Yet Eminently Curable Part II, 19 Green Bag 2d 257 (2016)

Judicial opinions and oral arguments

Alliance to End Repression v. Chicago,
   733 F.2d 1187 (7th Cir. 1984)
Atkins v. City of Chicago, 631 F.3d 823 (7th Cir. 2011)
Association of Administrative Law Judges v. Colvin,
   777 F.3d 402 (7th Cir. 2015) (Oral argument Dec. 9, 2014)
Attorney Registration & Disciplinary Commission v.
   Schweiker, 715 F.2d 282 (7th Cir. 1983)
Autotrol Corp. v. Continental Water Systems Corp.,
   918 F.2d 689 (7th Cir. 1990)

BIBLIOGRAPHY

Avitia v. Metropolitan Club, 49 F.3d 1219 (7th Cir. 1995)
Azeez v. Fairman, 795 F.2d 1296 (7th Cir. 1986)
Baskin v. Bogan (Oral argument Aug. 26, 2014)
Blue Canary Corp. v. City of Milwaukee,
 251 F.3d 1121 (7th Cir. 2001)
Bradford v. Brown, 831 F.3d 902 (7th Cir. 2016)
Colby v. J.C. Penney Co., 811 F.2d 1119 (7th Cir. 1987)
Cole v. Colvin, 831 F.3d 411 (7th Cir. 2016)
Del Raine v. Carlson, 826 F.2d 698 (7th Cir. 1987)
Discount Inn, Inc. v. City of Chicago,
 803 F.3d 317 (7th Cir. 2015)
Door Sys. v. Pro-Line Door Sys., 83 F.3d 169 (7th Cir. 1996)
Douglass v. Hustler Magazine, 769 F.2d 1128 (1985)
Employers Ins. of Wausau v. Titan Int'l,
 400 F.3d 486 (7th Cir. 2005)
Fuller v. Lynch, 833 F.3d 866 (7th Cir. 2016)
 (dissenting opinion)
Fox Valley AMC/Jeep, Inc. v. AM Credit Corp.,
 836 F.2d 366 (7th Cir. 1988)
Grip-Pak, Inc. v. Illinois Tool Works, Inc.,
 694 F.2d 466 (7th Cir. 1982)
Hartmann v. Prudential Ins. Co. of America,
 9 F.3d 1207 (7th Cir. 1993)
Hugunin v. Land O' Lakes Tackle Co.,
 815 F.3d 1064 (7th Cir. 2016)
Illinois v. General Electric Co., 683 F.2d 206 (7th Cir. 1982)
Illinois Transp. Trade Association v. Chicago,
 839 F.3d 594 (7th Cir. 2016)
In re Hoskins, 102 F.3d 311 (1996)
Jack Walters & Sons Corp. v. Morton Bldg., Inc.,
 737 F.2d 698 (7th Cir. 1984)
Kennedy v. Huibregtse, 831 F.3d 441 (7th Cir. 2016)
McDonald v. Schweiker, 726 F.2d 311 (7th Cir. 1983)
McKeever v. Israel, 689 F.2d 1315 (7th Cir. 1982)
Mei v. Ashcroft, 393 F.3d 737 (7th Cir. 2004)
Nicolet Instrument Corp. v. Lindquist & Vennum,
 34 F.3d 453 (7th Cir. 1994)
Parvati Corp. v. City of Oak Forest, 709 F.3d 678 (7th Cir. 2013)

Peaceable Planet, Inc. v. Ty, Inc., 362 F.3d 986 (7th Cir. 2004)
Reimnitz v. State's Attorney of Cook County,
    761 F.2d 405 (7th Cir. 1985)
Rowe v. Gibson, 798 F.3d 622 (7th Cir. 2015)
Samuel C. Johnson 1988 Trust v. Bayfield County,
    649 F.3d 799 (7th Cir. 2011)
Savage v. CIA, 826 F.2d 561 (7th Cir. 1987)
Schurz Communications v. FCC, 982 F.2d 1043 (7th Cir. 1992)
Shager v. Upjohn Co., 913 F.2d 398 (7th Cir. 1990)
Stuart v. Local 727, International Brotherhood of Teamsters,
    771 F.3d 1014 (7th Cir. 2014)
Taylor v. Colvin, 829 F.3d 799 (7th Cir. 2016)
United States *ex rel.* Bogina v. Medline Indus.,
    809 F.3d 365 (7th Cir. 2016)
United States v. Carson, 821 F.3d 849 (7th Cir. 2016)
    (dissenting opinion)
United States v. Cunningham, 103 F.3d 553 (7th Cir. 1996)
United States v. Dessart , 823 F.3d 395 (7th Cir. 2016)
    (concurring opinion)
United States v. Herrera-Medina, 853 F.2d 564 (7th Cir. 1988)
United States v. Miller, 832 F.3d 703 (7th Cir. 2016)
United States v. Tucker, 773 F.2d 136 (7th Cir. 1985)
Univ. of Notre Dame v. Sebelius (Oral argument Feb. 12, 2014)
Voices for Choices v. Illinois Bell Telephone Co.,
    339 F.3d 542 (7th Cir. 2003)
Voigt v. Colvin, 781 F.3d 871 (7th Cir. 2015)
Welge v. Planters Lifesavers Co., 17 F.3d 209 (1994)
Wolf v. Walker (Oral argument Aug. 26, 2014)
Wolin v. Smith Barney Inc., 83 F.3d 847 (7th Cir. 1996)

By others: books

Blomquist, Robert F. The Quotable Judge Posner, Selections
    from Twenty-Five Years of Judicial Opinions (1996)
Domnarski, William. Richard Posner (2016)

BIBLIOGRAPHY

Articles

Above the Law, *The Benchslap Dispatches: Posner v. Scalia — Is It Personal?*, Above the Law (Sept. 5, 2012), bit.ly/2gkQuHo

Bashman, Howard. *20 Questions for Circuit Judge Richard A. Posner of the U.S. Court of Appeals for the Seventh Circuit* (Dec. 1, 2003), bit.ly/HowAppealing_Posner

Charney, Noah. *How I Write: Richard Posner*, Daily Beast (Nov. 7, 2013)

Cohen, Joel. *An Interview With Judge Richard A. Posner*, ABA Journal (July 2014)

Collins, Ronald K.L. *The Man Behind the Robes — A Q&A with Richard Posner*, Concurring Opinions (Dec. 1, 2014), bit.ly/Collins3

Collins, Ronald K.L. *The Judge & Company – Questions for Judge Posner from Judges, Law Professors & a Journalist*, Concurring Opinions (Dec. 3, 2014), bit.ly/Collins4

A Conversation with Judge Richard A. Posner, 58 Duke L. J. 1807 (2009)

Coyne, Jerry. *Readers' cats: Pixie*, Why Evolution is True, bit.ly/PixieP

Judge Richard Posner Corrects The Record Regarding His Supreme Court Comments, Above the Law (Oct. 28, 2016), bit.ly/2gxFuEq

Kauper, Thomas. *Review of* Antitrust Law: An Economic Perspective *by Richard Posner*, 8 Bell J. Econ. & Mgmt. Sci. 609 (1977)

The Second Life of Judge Richard A. Posner (Dec. 11, 2006), bit.ly/Posner2dLife

Segall, Eric. *Judge Richard Posner, U.S. Court of Appeals for the Seventh Circuit*, New York Review of Books 47 (Sept. 29, 2011)

Tillman, Zoe. *Q&A: Judge Posner on Writing, Law School, and Cat Videos*, National Law Journal (May 18, 2016)

Totenberg, Nina. *Federal Judge Richard Posner: The GOP Has Made Me Less Conservative*, NPR (July 5, 2012), bit.ly/RAP-Goofy

Audio and video materials

BookTV, William Domnarski discusses Richard Posner, CSPAN (Oct. 4, 2016), cs.pn/2gxLY6p

First Amendment Salon (May 16, 2016), youtu.be/BTMT9Bf5qXU

Pearson v. Callahan, 555 U.S. 223 (2009) (Oral argument Oct. 6, 2009), www.oyez.org/cases/2008/07-751

INDEX

Adele, 9, 13, 37
Alito, Samuel, 72, 78
American Bar Association, 11
Amici curiae, 17, 135
AT&T, 9
Brennan, William, 8
Brontosauruses, 33
Canons of construction, 115
Cats, 15, 34, 43, 82
    cat's-paw theory, 21
    Maine Coon, 33, 113
    roughness of tongues, 20
    videos of, 84
    wisdom of, 85
Cavett, Dick, 5
Common law, 114
Constitution, U.S.
    study of, 112
Constructive possession, 119
Criticism, 20
Dancing, nude, 17
    strip joints, 17
Deference, 19
Dictionaries, 113
District courts, 49, 50
Dogs, 45, 61, 86
    cartoon, 140
    poodles, stabbing, 34

Dracula, 5
Emotional distress, 109
Eskimos, 32
Ethics, 37
    triviality of, 4
Exclamation points, 88
Experts, 47, 49, 108
    need for, 116
Fashion models. *See* law clerks
Federal Circuit, 118
Fiction
    humorous, 16
    popular, 15
Fourth Amendment, 108
Friendly, Henry, 7, 22, 26, 88
Garner, Bryan, 114
Google, 29, 31, 40, 47, 135
    hits, 30
Griswold, Erwin, 5
Hand, Learned, 26
Harvard
    College, 82
    Law Review, 6
    Law School, 5
Hearsay, 117
Holmes, Oliver Wendell Jr., 132
    crawling inside of, 16
    length of neck, 79, 80
Homosexuals, 32
    lesbians, 32

Internet research, 48, 115, 116
Judges
    ALJs, 36
    district court, 36
    immigration, 36
    new, 36
Juries, 42, 115
    instructions, 115
Kagan, Elena, 73
Las Vegas, 54
Law clerks, 31, 55, 57, 125
    career, 126
    exploding offers, 126
    mine, 127, 128
    personality, 127
    writing, 128, 129
Legal doctrine, 112
Magna Carta, 112
Monsters, 14
Narrow tailoring, 41
Obama, Barack, 6
Oral advocates. *See* Dogs
Oral argument, 42, 43, 44, 46
    advocates, 45
Originalism, 113
Parties, cocktail, 13
Patent law, 118
Philosophy, 36
Plain meaning, 25, 47
Poker, 55
Posner, Pixie, 71, 82, 83, 84, 86, 128, *See also* Cats, Maine Coon
    sound of purring, 85

Posner, Richard
    citations to, 20
    writing, 23
Precedent, 18, 41, 118
Preschool, 2, 68
Prisoner cases, 49
Privacy, 33, 135, 139
Raccoons, 31
Razors, 34, 35
Roberts, John, 69, 111
Sandwiches
    taco bowls as, 114
    tacos, 35
Scalia, Antonin, 71, 113, 114
    death of, 70
Senate
    confirmation hearing, 11
Sotomayor, Sonia, 73
Standards of review, 117, 120
Supreme Court, 7, 8, 20
    certiorari, 73
    clerkship, 6, 8
    partying, 55
    sexting, 69
Swift, Taylor, 13, 122
Sycophants, 15
Terrorism, 139
Textualism, 113
Theology, 17
Twitter, 14
Weeds, 35
Wikipedia, 116
Yale
    College, 3, 4
    Law School, 5

ABOUT @POSNER_THOUGHTS

Have you been paying attention at all?

ABOUT JACK METZLER

Jack Metzler is an attorney in Washington D.C. specializing in appellate and Supreme Court practice. As an oral advocate in the Supreme Court, he has achieved the same win-loss record as the Great Chief Justice John Marshall and President Abraham Lincoln: 0-1. See *Pearson v. Callahan*, 555 U.S. 223 (2009); *Williamson v. Barrett*, 13 How. 101 (1852); *Ware v. Hylton*, 3 Dall. 199 (1796). His record before Judge Posner (zero arguments) is also 0-1 (despite that the brief had a picture in it—go figure).

His other accomplishments include, *inter alia*, surfing in three oceans, having a solo show of his paintings in a D.C. gallery, and winning $150 one year when he bought a lottery ticket on his birthday (an economically irrational decision on multiple levels). He once memorized the Periodic Table of the Elements for fun. He is confident that—like Marshall and Lincoln after *their* Supreme Court arguments—the best is yet to come. Follow him on Twitter @SCOTUSPlaces.

www.ingramcontent.com/pod-product-compliance
Lightning Source LLC
Chambersburg PA
CBHW061604110426
42742CB00039B/2768